East Timor: Genocide in Paradise

Second Edition

Matthew Jardine

Introduction by Noam Chomsky

Odonian Press
distributed through
Common Courage Press / LPC Group

10/00

Additional copies of this and other Odonian Press Real Story books are available at most good bookstores, or directly from Common Courage Press. For a list of other titles, and details on ordering, see the inside back cover. To order by credit card, or for information on quantity discounts, please:
- call 207 525 0900 or 800 497 3207
- fax 207 525 3068
- email *odonian@realstory.com*
- visit the Odonian website at *www.realstory.com*
- write Common Courage at Box 702, Monroe ME 04951

Distribution to the book trade is through LPC Group, 1436 W. Randolph St, Chicago IL 60607. To order, call 800 243 0138. Real Story books are also available through wholesalers.

Organization and editing: **Sandy Niemann** *(lst edition),* **Arthur Naiman** *(both editions)*

Copyediting and proofreading: **Susan McCallister**

Index: **Steve Rath**   *Cover photograph:* **Elaine Brière**

Design and page layout: **Arthur Naiman**

Fonts: **Basilia** *(text),* **Liberty** *(headers, footers, titles),* **Optima** *(lists, notes, index, etc.),* **Dorovar** *(dedication)*

Series editor: **Arthur Naiman**

An Odonian Press Real Story book
published through Common Courage Press / LPC Group

Odonian Press gets its name from Ursula Le Guin's wonderful novel *The Dispossessed* (though we have no connection with Ms. Le Guin or any of her publishers). The last story in her collection *The Wind's Twelve Quarters* also features the Odonians (and Odo herself).

Odonian Press donates at least 10% of its aftertax income to organizations working for social justice.

C O N T E N T S

Dedicated to Tilson, Tima and all the other children of East Timor and Indonesia.

May they someday know a world of peace and justice.

ACKNOWLEDGMENTS

There are many people to whose work and assistance I owe a great debt and who have made this project possible. Given the limits of space and—more significantly—of my memory, there are surely many that I neglect. I am appreciative nonetheless.

I would like to thank Elaine Brière, Carmel Budiardjo, Roger Clark, James Dunn, Carol and Ping Ferry, Lynn Fredriksson, Geoffrey Gunn, Gerry Hale, William Hartung, Bruno Kahn, Liem Soei Liong, Andrew McNaughtan, John Miller, Josh Muldavin, Constâncio Pinto, Ben Terrall, Manija Said, Sharon Scharfe, Charlie Scheiner, Jennifer Washburn, David Webster, Rob Wesley Smith and friends from the CNRT for all their support and assistance.

I am very grateful to Mizue Aizeki, Martin Ang, Allan Nairn and Mark Salzer for having read early drafts of the first edition of the book and for their critical and helpful comments.

I also want to extend my gratitude to Sandy Niemann for her careful editing of the first edition, and to Arthur Naiman for his professional and political commitment to this project and for all his work in making both editions possible.

I especially want to thank Mizue for her love and patience, and my parents for their infinite support.

Finally, I want to thank all those of East Timor and Indonesia who continue to struggle for basic human rights, human dignity and democracy. Your example inspires me and countless others throughout the world to work to claim our own humanity.

Matthew Jardine

P R E F A C E

The island of Timor lies about four hundred miles northwest of Australia and about a thousand miles due south of the southern tip of the Philippines. It's slightly larger than the state of Maryland, and most of its terrain is mountainous.

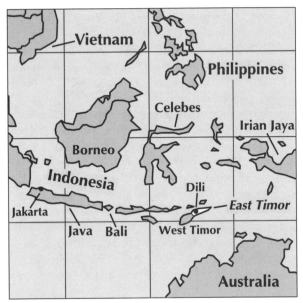

From the early 1600s, the Portuguese and Dutch fought over Timor. Eventually, they divided it, with the Portuguese getting the eastern part and the Dutch the western part.

When the Dutch East Indies won their independence and became Indonesia in 1949, West Timor was absorbed into the new nation. East Timor remained a Portuguese colony until the mid-1970s, when Portugal's overseas empire began to fall apart.

East Timor declared its independence on November 28, 1975. But it didn't stay independent for long. Unfortunately for the tiny nation's dreams of freedom, Indonesia controlled not only West Timor but virtually every other nearby island as well.

Most Americans don't realize how large Indonesia is. More than 200 million people now live on its 17,000 islands; only China, India and the US have larger populations. (The capital, Jakarta, is on the island of Java, where about 60% of Indonesia's population lives.)

Indonesia's army and government are among the most brutal in the world. In 1965, under General Suharto, the army—and civilian death squads affiliated with it—slaughtered more than a million alleged enemies of the state (including women and children) in just a few months.

The generals who run Indonesia aren't interested in self-determination, human rights or other wimpy, democratic ideals. They're interested in maintaining control over their vast territory and plundering it for as much profit as they can—almost always with the help of Western or Japanese partners.

Just nine days after East Timor declared its independence—and just hours after US President Ford and Secretary of State Kissinger ended a festive two-day visit with Indonesia's dictator, General Suharto—Indonesia invaded East Timor. It was December 7, 1975, and like the attack on Pearl Harbor on the same date in 1941, it's a day that will live in infamy.

In the first few weeks of the invasion, Indonesian troops killed tens of thousands of people (not surprising, given their record). But the genocidal war of occupation Indonesia has been waging ever since the invasion has broken new ground, even for them.

In 1975, East Timor had a population of about 690,000. Since then, more than 200,000 East Timorese have died as a result of the Indonesian occupation.

In this book, Matthew Jardine and Noam Chomsky tell the story of East Timor's heroic struggle against impossible odds. They also explain why you hardly ever hear about East Timor in the western media—and why, when the Indonesian army murders someone there, you and I pay for the bullets they use.

Arthur Naiman

I N T R O D U C T I O N
Noam Chomsky

In the annals of crime of this terrible century, Indonesia's assault against East Timor ranks high, not only because of its scale—perhaps the greatest death toll relative to the population since the Holocaust—but because it would have been so easy to prevent, and to bring to an end at any time. There is no need for threats to bomb Jakarta, or even to impose sanctions on the aggressor. It would suffice for the great powers to refrain from their eager participation in Indonesia's crimes—to stop putting guns into the hands of the killers and torturers while joining them in robbery of the off-shore oil of the Timor Gap.

Two years ago, Indonesian Foreign Minister Ali Alatas said that his government faced an important choice on East Timor, which had become "like a sharp piece of gravel in our shoes." Benedict Anderson, a leading specialist on Indonesia, took this to be one of many signs of second thoughts: "Alatas doesn't spell out what the choice is," Anderson commented, "but he's implying you should take your shoe off and get rid of the gravel."

The gravel was not sharpened by Western power. Quite the contrary: the West and Japan have been willing partners in Indonesia's conquest and annexation of the former Portuguese colony. Well before Indonesia began its campaign of sub-version and terror in 1975, followed by direct invasion on December 7, the British Embassy in Jakarta reported that, "Certainly as seen from here, it is in Britain's interest that Indonesia should absorb the territory as soon as and as unobtrusively as possible; and that if it comes to the crunch and there is a row in the United Nations, we should keep our heads down and avoid siding against the Indonesian government."

Australia shared this judgment. In August 1975, Ambassador to Jakarta Richard Woolcott advised in secret cables that Australia take "a prag-matic rather than a principled stand" with regard to the forthcoming invasion because "that is what national interest and foreign policy is all about." Along with the ritual reference to "the Australian defence interest," Woolcott suggested that a favorable treaty on the Timor Gap "could be much more readily negotiated with Indonesia...than with Portugal or independent Portuguese Timor." He recommended a preference for "Kissingerian realism" over "Wilsonian idealism"—a distinction that can perhaps be detected in actual practice, with a powerful enough microscope.

The reasons for support for Indonesia's crimes went well beyond oil and "defence interests," including control of a deep-water passage for nuclear submarines. Indonesia has been an honored ally ever since General Suharto came to power in 1965 with a "boiling bloodbath" that was "the West's best news for years in Asia" *(Time),* a "staggering mass slaughter of Communists and pro-Communists," mostly landless peasants, that provided a "gleam of light in Asia" *(New York Times).*

Euphoria knew no bounds, along with praise for the "Indonesian moderates" who prevailed *(New York Times)* and their leader, who is "at heart benign" *(The Economist).* Not only did the welcome bloodbath destroy the only mass-based political party in Indonesia, but it opened the rich resources of the country to Western exploitation and even justified the American war in Vietnam, which "provided a shield for the sharp reversal of Indonesia's shift toward Communism," as Freedom House soberly explained with no reservations. Such favors are not quickly forgotten.

Woolcott offered some illustrations of "Kissingerian realism." Noting with diplomatic understatement that "the United States might have some influence on Indonesia at present," he

9

reported that Kissinger had instructed US Ambassador David Newsom to avoid the Timor issue and cut down Embassy reporting, allowing "events to take their course." Newsom informed Woolcott that if Indonesia were to invade, the US hoped it would do so "effectively, quickly, and not use our equipment"—90% of its weapons supply.

Another lesson in realism was given by UN Ambassador Daniel Patrick Moynihan, celebrated for his courageous defense of international law and human rights. "The United States wished things to turn out as they did," he writes in his memoirs, "and worked to bring this about. The Department of State desired that the United Nations prove utterly ineffective in whatever measures it undertook. This task was given me, and I carried it forward with no inconsiderable success." Moynihan cites figures of 60,000 killed in the first few months, "almost the proportion of casualties experienced by the Soviet Union during the Second World War," a foretaste of still greater successes soon to come.

Western governments were fully aware of what was happening throughout, contrary to subsequent pretense. As revealed in leaked internal records, Kissinger's worst fear was that his complicity in the aggression might become public, and "used against me" by real or imagined political enemies. Cable traffic shows that after "Suharto was given the green light," the main concern of the Embassy and State Department was "about the problems that would be created for us if the public and Congress became aware" of the American role, according to Philip Liechty, then a senior CIA officer in Jakarta.

Weapons provided by the US were limited strictly to self-defense. That posed no problem for Kissingerian realism: "And we can't construe a Communist government in the middle of Indonesia as self-defense?" Kissinger asked with derision when the question was raised in internal discussion. An independent East Timor would be "Communist" by the usual criteria: it might not follow orders in a sprightly enough manner, interfering with the "national interest." New arms were sent, including counterinsurgency equipment; "everything that you need to fight a major war against somebody who doesn't have any guns," Liechty comments, adding that the advanced military equipment proved decisive, as other sources confirm.

Had there been a challenge, ample precedent could have been cited. "Great souls care little for small morals," another statesman observed two centuries ago.

By 1977, Indonesia found itself short of weapons, an indication of the scale of its attack. The Carter administration accelerated the arms flow. Britain joined in as atrocities peaked in 1978, while France announced that it would sell arms to Indonesia and protect it from any public "embarrassment." Others too sought to gain what profit they could from the slaughter and torture of Timorese.

The press added its contribution. Coverage of East Timor in the United States had been high in 1974–75, amidst concerns over the break-up of the Portuguese empire. As another "boiling blood-bath" proceeded, coverage declined, keeping largely to the lies and apologetics of the State Department and Indonesian generals. By 1978, as the slaughter reached genocidal levels, coverage reached flat zero. The same was true in Canada, another leading supporter of Indonesia.

In 1990, the issue of Timor received some attention when Iraq invaded Kuwait, eliciting a response from the West rather unlike its reaction to Indonesia's vastly more bloody invasion and annexation of a small oil-rich country next door. Much ingenuity was displayed in explaining that the distinction did not lie in the locus of power and profit, but in some more subtle quality that preserves Anglo-American virtue. Similar gyrations had been undertaken a decade earlier to justify the radically different reaction to simultaneous atrocities in Cambodia and Timor; crucially different, to be sure, in that the latter could have been readily terminated.

Some commentators were forthright. Australian Foreign Minister Gareth Evans explained in 1990 that "the world is a pretty unfair place, littered with examples of acquisition by force." Since "there is no binding legal obligation not to recognize the acquisition of territory that was acquired by force," Australia may proceed to share Timor's oil with the conqueror. The dispensation would presumably not have extended to a Libya-Iraq treaty on Kuwait oil. Meanwhile Prime Minister Hawke declared that "big countries cannot invade small neighbors and get away with it" (referring to Iraq and Kuwait); "would-be aggressors will think twice before invading smaller neighbors," secure in the lesson that "the rule of law must prevail over the rule of force in international relations"—at least, when the "national interest" so dictates.

The Timor issue reached threshold again in November 1991, when Indonesian troops attacked a graveyard commemoration of an earlier assassination, massacring hundreds of people and severely beating two US reporters. The tactical error called for the standard cover-up, deemed satisfactory by Western leaders. Oil exploration proceeded on course, contracts with Australian, British, Japanese, Dutch and American companies were reported in the six months following the massacre. "To the capitalist governors," a Timorese priest wrote, "Timor's petroleum smells better than Timorese blood and tears."

The primary reason why Indonesia might consider "taking the shoe off" is given in the final words of the powerful and revealing chapters on Timor in the 1994 edition of John Pilger's *Distant Voices.* The reason is "the enduring heroism of the people of East Timor, who continue to resist invaders even as the crosses multiply on the hillsides," a constant "reminder of the fallibility of brute power and of the cynicism of others."

However courageous they may be, the people of East Timor have no hope without outside support. No amount of courage and unity will prevent Indonesian transmigration, atrocities and destruction of the indigenous culture, funded and supported by the great powers.

Though the pace has been glacial, support for Timorese rights has finally reached a significant level in the United States. The truth began to seep into the public domain, compelling the media to take some notice and raising impediments to the "pragmatic course."

A headline in the *Boston Globe* on the anniversary of the 1991 massacre reads: "Indonesian general, facing suit, flees Boston." Sent to study at Harvard after the massacre, the general was charged in a suit on behalf of a woman whose son was among those murdered in the graveyard—many more afterwards, as revealed by Pilger and the courageous Indonesian academic George Aditjondro, who released investigations based on 20 years research that supports the most gruesome estimates of atrocities. Popular awareness and activism have become strong enough so that favored mass murders can no longer find a comfortable refuge in the United States, as had been learned a year earlier by one of Guatemala's leading killers, General Hector Gramajo, in a similar manner.

Congress has imposed barriers on military aid and training, which the White House has had to evade in ever more devious ways, particularly in recent months. Sensing the opportunity, Britain moved effectively under Thatcher's guiding hand to take first place in the highly profitable enterprise of war crimes. As explained by Defense Procurement Minister Alan Clark, "I don't really fill my mind much with what one set of foreigners is doing to another" when there is money to be made by arms sales. We must insist on "reserving the right to bomb niggers," as Lloyd George recognized 60 years ago.

John Pilger's recent work, including the remarkable documentary based on his visit to East Timor, threatens to arouse the Western public to a heightened awareness of what is being perpetrated in their names. Its great significance is attested by the angry response it has evoked from high government officials. To draw aside the veils of deceit that conceal the real world is no small achievement. But it will join other failed efforts unless the public response goes beyond mere awareness, to actions to end shameful complicity in crime.

Noam Chomsky
Originally published in The Guardian *(London), 7/5/94*

THE SANTA CRUZ MASSACRE

On November 12, 1991, a crowd of mourners gathered at a local parish church in East Timor's capital, Dili. They'd come to attend a memorial mass for Sebastiao Gomes, a pro-independence activist who had been killed at that same church by Indonesian soldiers two weeks earlier.

Such killings had become common occurrences since the Indonesian invasion. But this particular day of mourning would have special significance—in large part because journalists from the US and Great Britain were there to report it.

When the mass ended, a procession began to the Santa Cruz Cemetery, about a mile away. Although Indonesian soldiers lined the streets, the mourners unfurled banners and shouted pro-independence slogans. This uncharacteristically open defiance of Indonesian authority caught the attention of those whose homes and places of work lined the procession route. Supporters joined in, and soon the crowd had swelled to thousands.

At the cemetery, some of the crowd went to the gravesite with Sebastiao's family. Others waited outside the walls. They were the first to notice that Indonesian army trucks had blocked the road back to town, and that a column of armed soldiers was slowly making its way toward the crowd.

Veteran US journalist Allan Nairn, an eyewitness, reports what happened next:

[Without warning, and without provocation], soldiers raised their rifles, and took aim. Then, acting in unison, they opened fire....Men and women fell, shivering, in the street, rolling from the impact of the bullets. Some were backpedalling, and tripping, their hands held up. Others simply tried to turn and run. The soldiers jumped over fallen bodies and fired at the people still upright. They chased down young boys and girls and shot them in the back.

When it was over, more than 250 people had been killed and hundreds more wounded. (The soldiers also badly beat Nairn and fellow US journalist Amy Goodman.)

Max Stahl, a British journalist whose video camera captured the horror, called it a "cold-blooded and premeditated massacre." Eyewitnesses told him that Indonesian soldiers killed many of the wounded at the military hospital in Dili; they "crushed the skulls of the wounded with large rocks, ran over them with trucks, stabbed them and administered—with doctors present—poisonous disinfecting chemicals as medicines." Stahl estimates that 50–200 of the wounded died in this way.

When news of the Santa Cruz massacre appeared in the Western media, it sparked international outrage. The US Congress and European Parliament passed resolutions condemning Indonesia, and the Netherlands, Denmark and Canada suspended aid. Editorials favoring East Timorese self-determination appeared in newspapers throughout the West.

Indonesia moved swiftly to stifle the criticism. It expressed official "regret" for what had happened, set up an official investigation of the incident, relieved the two top military commanders for East Timor (sending them abroad for "study") and sentenced a few low-ranking officers for ostensibly disobeying orders. It also sent its foreign minister on a tour of the US, Canada and Western Europe to repair Indonesia's damaged reputation (demonstrations plagued him wherever he went).

But the words of two top-ranking military officials undoubtedly expressed Jakarta's real sentiments. General Try Sutrisno, the commander of the Indonesian military at the time of the massacre and later the country's vice-president, said that the East Timorese who'd gathered at the cemetery were "disrupters" who "must be crushed." He added, "Delinquents like these have to be shot, and we will shoot them."

General Mantiri, regional commander for East Timor just after the Santa Cruz massacre, declared that the massacre was "proper" and added: "We don't regret anything." That lack of regret was clear from the sentences meted out to participants in the Santa Cruz march and to East Timorese demonstrators in Jakarta who protested the massacre. They ranged from five years to life imprisonment.

Despite the media coverage the Santa Cruz massacre received in the Western media, you can still go months without hearing a word about East Timor and the people who are dying there.

PORTUGUESE RULE

East Timor, under the Portuguese, seemed to sit still in history. The clock of development didn't tick there.

Nobel Peace Prize winner José Ramos-Horta

Portuguese traders arrived on Timor around 1515, anxious to take advantage of the island's already lucrative sandalwood trade. Timorese leaders on the coast exchanged sandalwood brought from the mountainous interior for Portuguese guns, cloth and iron tools.

In the beginning, these Portuguese visits had little effect on the Timorese. Most of the islanders lived in small, relatively isolated villages in the interior, where subsistence agriculture and animist religions predominated.

Eventually, however, the European influence became more invasive. In the late 1500s, Dominican friars from Portugal established a mission in the major sandalwood port. Not long after that, the *Topasses,* or Black Portuguese—the offspring of Portuguese soldiers, sailors and traders and women from neighboring islands— began to settle on Timor. They spread Portuguese culture and influence, and soon controlled the local trading networks.

Soon afterwards, the Dutch began visiting Timor, to obtain sandalwood and slaves. The two colonial powers were soon in conflict, as each tried to extend its influence on the island. The next two centuries were dominated by power struggles between the colonial powers, the *Topasses* and indigenous Timorese. The official division of the island into West (Dutch) Timor and East (Portuguese) Timor wasn't formalized until 1913.

In the first 300 years of colonial rule, Portugal showed less interest in East Timor than in any of its other colonies. In the 1860s, Alfred R. Wallace, a British explorer, described the situation like this:

> The Portuguese government in Timor is a most miserable one. Nobody seems to care the least about the improvement of the country, and at this time, after three hundred years of occupation, there has not been a mile of road made beyond the town [Dili], and there is not a solitary European residence in the interior.

But by the end of the 19th century, this situation began to change rapidly. Portugal wanted to boost its economic power to catch up with its European rivals and to stave off threats to its colonies from Britain, Germany and France, who were looking to expand their empires.

Hoping that the colonies themselves could become a significant source of income for the mother country, Portugal began to increase the economic and social development of East Timor. This often entailed heavy-handed tactics like the forced cultivation of cash crops, forced labor to build the territory's infrastructure, and the levying of head taxes.

Such methods led to widespread resentment and finally large-scale violence, culminating in an uprising that began in 1910, led by a local ruler. By 1912, the rebellion threatened Portuguese control of Dili itself, but it was violently suppressed with the aid of African troops from the Portuguese colony of Mozambique.

At the same time, the Portuguese administration began cultivating a town-based elite of native East Timorese in order to fill the new administrative, managerial and service-oriented jobs that were being generated by development. These jobs required both education and a colonial perspective, and the Catholic Church helped cultivate both. By 1900, it was running twenty schools that emphasized Portuguese language, geography and culture.

Despite these development efforts, Timor never became much of an economic asset to Portugal. In fact, it remained one of the most economically backward colonies in all of Southeast Asia. As one historian described it:

> On the eve of World War II the capital, Dili, had no electricity and no town water supply; there were no paved roads, no telephone services (other than to the houses and offices of senior officials), and not even a wharf for cargo handling.

World War II was to bring even the modest efforts Portugal was making to modernize East Timor to an abrupt standstill.

WORLD WAR II AND AFTER

When the Western allies declared war against Japan, they decided to use the island of Timor as a line of defense against Japan's southward advance (despite protests from the neutral Portuguese). By mid-December 1941, just ten days after Pearl Harbor, about 400 Dutch East Indies and Australian troops landed west of Dili.

Two months later, Japan attacked the island, and quickly drove the Dutch out of the western half. In East Timor, a few hundred Australian commandos and some Timorese managed to hold about 20,000 Japanese soldiers at bay for almost a year. But by January 1943, the Japanese controlled the entire island.

The Japanese occupation was one of the darkest times in East Timor's history (though its cruelty and devastation has been surpassed by the Indonesians). Here's how Iwamura Shouachi, who commanded a Japanese platoon in East Timor for over two years, described the hardships the Japanese military imposed:

> It is painful to speak today of the sacrifices and burdens we forced upon the East Timorese.... We ordered chiefs to mobilize people *en masse* for road construction...to work without receiving food or compensation. Because of food shortage [sic] people died of starvation every day. Food for Japanese soldiers and horses to transport ammunition were confiscated from the people, and some of the troops under my command raped Timorese women.

Had the Australians and the Allies left the island alone, the Japanese might very well have

21

ignored Timor, or at most sent a token contingent of soldiers. But instead, about 60,000 East Timorese lost their lives as a result of the brutal Japanese occupation and the Allied bombing that aimed to dislodge it. The war badly damaged Dili and partly destroyed many of the territory's principal towns and villages.

With Japan's defeat in August 1945, Portugal returned and reasserted its control over East Timor, which gradually returned to its pre-war state. The Portuguese began to rebuild the devastated colonial infrastructure, often employing the same brutal methods and forced labor they'd used before the war.

With the exception of a serious revolt in 1959 (which was quickly put down), relations between the Timorese and the Portuguese remained fairly calm—though resentment simmered beneath the surface. The Catholic Church, whose membership had swelled because of the harrowing experiences of the war, helped smooth tensions by encouraging pro-Portuguese sentiment in worship and education.

Throughout Southeast Asia, the post-war era was one of great political upheaval, as colonized territories sought independence and as returning colonial powers tried to reassert their control. The people of the Dutch East Indies declared Indonesia to be a free country on August 17, 1945, while still under Japanese occupation.

When the Dutch returned, they refused to recognize this declaration of independence and instead waged a brutal military campaign to reclaim their colony. But by the end of 1949, massive resistance forced the Dutch to recognize the independence of Indonesia. The US government pressured the Dutch to do this, since it believed that a stable, independent Indonesia would provide a better business environment for US capital than a rebellious, war-torn colony.

In East Timor itself, post-war nationalism came more slowly, but it finally did come. By the late 1950s, public radio began broadcasting in Portuguese, Tetum (the *lingua franca* used by people who spoke different native languages) and Chinese (business in the colony was dominated by Chinese immigrants and by Timorese of Chinese descent). A government-controlled newspaper, *A Voz de Timor,* began publishing in 1960. Since both the radio and the newspaper were regularly censored by authorities, however, they offered only limited exposure to "foreign" ideas.

Certain elements in the Catholic Church played an important role in facilitating nationalistic thinking. Although most Catholic schools focussed on things Portuguese, the Jesuits were often critical of colonialism and of social conditions. In their seminary outside Dili, where many of the East Timorese who worked for the Portuguese administration received their education, Jesuit teachers discussed burgeoning nationalist movements and progressive approaches to Third World development, and promoted a sense of Timorese identity among their students.

A church newspaper, *Seara,* which was free from censorship laws, taught Tetum to its readers and sometimes served as a lively forum for progressive ideas. Some of its contributors, who'd had contact with African liberation movements, began to privately advocate East Timor's independence. The Portuguese authorities forced *Seara* to stop publication in 1973, but by that time like-minded dissidents were already meeting clandestinely with one another in Dili.

Although the vast majority of the population still lived as they had for centuries in rural hamlets, a small, educated elite had developed by the 1970s. When the Portuguese empire finally began to crumble, this group of students, teachers and even colonial administrators helped tiny East Timor emerge from its relative isolation into the turbulent world of international power politics.

THE STRUGGLE FOR INDEPENDENCE

Don't dream about having...a state of Timtim [the Indonesian name for East Timor]. *There is no such thing!....From now on, Timtim is the same as other regions. So don't try to be latter-day heroes, beating your breasts and proclaiming, 'I am a Timtim patriot.' There is no such thing as a Timtim nation, there is only an Indonesian nation....*

If you try to make your own state...it will be crushed by [the Indonesian military]....There have been bigger rebellions, there have been greater differences of opinion with the government than the small number calling themselves FRETILIN, or whoever their sympathizers are here. We will crush them all! I repeat, we will crush them all!

Indonesian Defense Minister Benny Murdani,
speaking in Dili, February 1990

In late April 1974, a group of left-leaning military officers stationed in Lisbon (Portugal's capital) overthrew the country's fascist government in a

relatively bloodless coup. There was some dis-
agreement among the officers (who called themselves the Armed Forces Movement, or MFA)
about what to do with Portugal's colonies. The
conservative head of the MFA favored what he
called "progressive autonomy...within a Portuguese framework," but other officers, many of
whom had recently returned from fighting liberation movements in the African colonies, champi-
oned "some form of independence."

In June 1974, Portugal laid out three possible
options for East Timor: continued association
with Portugal, independence, or becoming part of
Indonesia. But the Portuguese government took
no immediate action on any of these options.

In East Timor itself, however, the response to
the coup was much less sluggish. Within little
more than a month, three political parties had
formed: the UDT, the ASDT (which later became
FRETILIN) and APODETI.

The first party founded, the UDT (the Timorese Democratic Union), was generally conservative and pro-Portuguese. It initially advocated
continued ties with Lisbon, but as opposition to
colonialism mounted, it soon began supporting
the idea of eventual total independence.

The second party founded, the ASDT (the
Association of Timorese Social Democrats), advocated "the universal doctrines of socialism and
democracy." Fully committed to independence
from the beginning, it envisioned an eight-to-ten-
year decolonization period in which the East
Timorese could develop the political and economic structures necessary for independence.

Both the UDT and the ASDT drew their leadership largely from the middle and upper classes— Timorese who had studied at the Jesuit college at Soibada and the seminary outside of Dili, and who were colonial administrators or school teachers. East Timor's wealthiest citizens tended to support the UDT. They included senior administrative officials, native leaders and prominent plantation owners. One UDT leader—its first president, in fact—was later appointed governor of East Timor by the Indonesians, a post he held from 1981 to 1992.

The third party, APODETI (the Timorese Popular Democratic Association) favored an "autonomous integration" with Indonesia. (Its original name—the Association for the Integration of Timor into Indonesia—was quickly changed for public-relations purposes.)

APODETI, which never had more than a few hundred members, soon came under the influence of the Indonesian military's intelligence service. The last thing Indonesia wanted was another independent country on its borders, and it was dedicated to making sure this never happened.

Three men who'd been cooperating with the Indonesian military for a number of years became key leaders in APODETI. And immediately after APODETI's founding, Indonesia began providing East Timorese agents with financial support.

UDT began as the largest and most popular group, but it soon began to lose ground to the ASDT, which was better organized and more innovative. When the deputy president of the Indonesian parliament said that he favored Indonesian control of East Timor, the ASDT sent an envoy, José Ramos-Horta, to Jakarta, where he was assured by Indonesia's foreign minister that Indonesia unequivocally supported East Timorese self-determination.

Next José Ramos-Horta went to Australia, but the Australian government was unwilling to meet with him or to make any official statement in favor of self-determination for East Timor. He did, however, get support from church groups, trade unionists, academics and members of parliament.

As its members—and the East Timorese population in general—became more radical, ASDT changed its name, in September 1974, to FRETILIN (the Revolutionary Front for an Independent East Timor) and demanded immediate independence from Portugal. FRETILIN volunteers began to move out from Dili into the rural areas, teaching villagers to read and write Tetum, establishing agricultural cooperatives, helping organize labor unions and other groups, and promoting local culture by encouraging the creation of nationalist poems, songs and dances. Thanks to these activities, FRETILIN became, by early 1975, the most popular of the three parties.

While Portugal's president called full East Timorese independence "unrealistic," the MFA's new governor of East Timor (and local MFA officers there) wanted to help the country gain its freedom. In December 1974, they invited the three parties to advise Lisbon on how to decolonize East Timor. The UDT and FRETILIN joined in the process and then formed a coalition. APODETI refused to participate, claiming it recognized only the Indonesian government, not the Portuguese.

In May 1975, the UDT, FRETILIN and the MFA agreed that a transitional government would be set up by October, and that elections for a national constituent assembly would be held in the fall of 1976. But Indonesia had different plans. By mid-1974, it had developed Operation Komodo—named after the Komodo dragons, giant man-eating lizards that live on other Indonesian islands.

Operation Komodo aimed to strengthen APODETI and weaken FRETILIN, and it scored a number of diplomatic successes. Meeting with Indonesian President Suharto in September 1974, Australian Prime Minister Gough Whitlam stated that an independent East Timor would be "unviable" and "a potential threat to the area." He voiced his support for a voluntary union between East Timor and Indonesia. Although he added that Australia wouldn't approve of the use of force in East Timor, his comments overall were seen by Jakarta as being very favorable to their position.

When FRETILIN and the UDT started to work together, Indonesia stepped up Operation Komodo. In mid-February 1975, the Indonesian military (commonly referred to by the acronym ABRI) staged exercises in Sumatra that simulated an air and sea attack on East Timor. Soon thereafter, Indonesia began disseminating false reports of a planned coup by the MFA and FRETILIN, and of supposed persecution of APODETI members.

Operation Komodo, combined with FRETILIN's growing popularity, weakened the UDT-FRETILIN coalition. Indonesia was able to convince the more conservative members of the UDT that international isolation would result if leftists were allowed to remain in the coalition.

In late May 1975, the UDT formally withdrew from the coalition.

UDT leaders met with Indonesian officials in Jakarta and became convinced that Indonesia wouldn't allow East Timorese independence under FRETILIN and probably not even under the UDT. They felt that only by purging the territory of "communist" influence would they have any chance of preventing an Indonesian invasion.

Finally, in mid-August 1975, Indonesia gave the UDT false intelligence reports of an imminent FRETILIN power grab, complete with clandestine Chinese arms shipments and "Vietnamese terrorists" entering East Timor to help FRETILIN. The UDT launched a coup, quickly capturing the communications station and the airport in Dili.

But the UDT greatly underestimated the strength of FRETILIN, which was able to persuade most East Timorese units in the Portuguese army to side with it. Soon FRETILIN controlled all of Dili and by late September it had driven 500 UDT soldiers and 2500 refugees (mostly family of UDT leaders and soldiers) into West Timor. The brief civil war was over.

(Indonesia permitted the refugees to enter West Timor only if they signed a petition calling for East Timor's integration into Indonesia. As a former UDT leader put it: "It was the last thing we wanted, but with FRETILIN forces closing in on us and without food, we really had no alternative but to agree.")

FRETILIN immediately began to set up a *de facto* government to fill in for the Portuguese, who had fled during the civil war. The former

Australian Consul in Dili, James Dunn, described the people's response:

> This administrative structure had obvious short-comings, but it clearly enjoyed widespread support or cooperation from the population, including many former UDT supporters....
>
> Indeed, the leaders of the victorious party were welcomed warmly and spontaneously in all main centers by crowds of Timorese. In my long association with the territory, I had never before witnessed such demonstrations of spontaneous warmth and support from the ordinary people.

In order to complete the process of decolonization, FRETILIN called for a peace conference that would include leaders from Portugal, Indonesia, East Timor and Australia, but Portugal's constant postponements prevented the talks from ever materializing. Meanwhile, ABRI (the Indonesian military) was making incursions over the border from West Timor, to give the appearance of an ongoing civil war. (Indonesia denied these incursions, but even the CIA confirmed them.)

ABRI soon captured some towns near the border between East and West Timor. Their campaign culminated in a two-week land, air and sea attack on a town called Atabae, just 35 miles from Dili. ABRI finally took Atabae on November 28th, 1975. Faced with an imminent, full-scale invasion, FRETILIN declared the independence of the Democratic Republic of East Timor that same day.

FRETILIN hoped this declaration would give East Timor some international protection, but only four former Portuguese colonies in Africa recognized the new country immediately. Western nations, which knew all about Indonesia's plans to invade, remained silent.

INDONESIA INVADES

The Indonesian forces are killing indiscriminately. Women and children are being shot in the streets. We are all going to be killed. I repeat, we are all going to be killed....This is an appeal for international help. Please do something to stop this invasion.

> FRETILIN radio broadcast from Dili
> in the early hours of December 7, 1975

The total may be 50,000, but what does this mean if compared with 600,000 people who want to join Indonesia? Then what is the big fuss? It is possible that they may have been killed by Australians and not us. Who knows? It was war.

> Indonesia's foreign minister, Adam Malik,
> referring to the number of East Timorese killed
> in the first fifteen months of the "civil war"

On December 7, 1975, the long-feared invasion began. At 2 am, Indonesian ships began to bombard the outskirts of Dili, where they thought FRETILIN's military wing, FALINTIL, had artillery batteries. By 5 am, planes were dropping paratroopers into the waterfront area.

ABRI soldiers began to rampage through the town. According to the former Catholic bishop of Dili, "The soldiers who landed started killing everyone they could find. There were many dead bodies in the streets—all we could see were the soldiers killing, killing, killing."

Eloise, an East Timorese living in Dili, awoke to the sounds of invading troops. She describes the atrocities that followed:

On 7 December we woke and heard this big noise of planes and saw parachutes and planes covering the light—it became dark because of them, so many. Then there were shots and we went inside and kept listening to more and more shooting. In the afternoon some Timorese came and told us everyone must come to surrender at headquarters....

Once we got there they divided us: the women and children and old men to one side, and on the other young boys [and men]....

Then an Indonesian screams an order and we hear machine guns running through the men. We see the boys and men dying right there. Some see their husbands die. We look at each other stunned. We think they are going to kill us next. All of us just turn and pick up the children and babies and run screaming, wild, everywhere....

[Later] my sister went to look for her husband and son. On her way she met a friend crying who told her, "Don't bother going there. I have just seen my cousin being eaten by a dog. They are all dead. Only the dogs are alive there."

Mr. Siong, a Chinese Timorese living near the harbor, reported similar atrocities:

At midday [on December 7] they take six of us [men] to work at the harbour....[where] we have to pick up...dead bodies....There were a lot of iron pipes on the wharf and we must tie the dead bodies on to them with parachute rope and throw them into the sea....

[Chinese Timorese from a Dili suburb] came in groups of two or three or four, stood on the wharf and were shot. One group after the other coming and coming, killed and thrown in the sea. Two were couples, one with young children who went with relatives. The other couple were elderly, and the rest were men....

Next they bring the ten [men who had been working with us]....The Indonesians tell them to stand in line and face the sea and then they are shot with a machine gun. Four people in that first sixteen of us...were father and son, but the Indonesians didn't know this. There on the wharf they kill the father, and the son must tie and throw his father into the sea. Then they kill the other son and his father is one of the six of us who must tie and throw his body.

After the initial mass killings, the soldiers began looting homes and churches, loading whatever they had stolen—furniture, cars, motorcycles and even windows—onto ships destined for Java (where most ABRI officers are based).

The ABRI troops also started looking for "girls." Olinda, a young Chinese Timorese woman reported what her uncle had seen:

After they landed in Dili the Indonesians....asked everywhere, "Where are the single girls? I want to marry," and this kind of thing. An uncle spoke Bahasa Indonesia [the official Indonesian language], for trade with West Timor. They forced him to go with them to interpret. He came back and told how the Indonesians were raping Timorese women.

Refugees reported soldiers raping women in front of their husbands or fathers, severely beating, imprisoning or sometimes even killing those men who refused to surrender their wives or daughters. Women and girls who were active in organizations linked to FRETILIN or relatives of FRETILIN members were subjected to the worst treatment. The soldiers arrested and imprisoned most of them; many were also repeatedly tortured and raped.

Many East Timorese fled to the mountains to avoid the oncoming troops. One of them, a woman named Edhina, described the situation:

> We were very frightened and ran to the bush....There were 40,000 of us, the fighters said. I had never seen so many people together....
>
> The Javanese kept attacking and dropping bombs and we were like animals running from one place to the other carrying our children, going this way and that way. We slept anywhere, in the rain, in the mud, even near the dead animals. The bombs would come and we would stand up and run again. On the way we ate anything growing, anything we could find. In the daytime we went into caves or under rocks to hide. We could come out at night to sleep in the open air and cook, make a hole and light a little fire without smoke, only coals.
>
> People and animals ran, pushed to the interior of the mountains where there was no water. In the beginning we could carry food but after a while we couldn't carry that and carry our children. We were running all the time and we were weaker. When people died, we'd just lay them next to the dead animals.

In the first two days of the invasion, 2,000 people in Dili were slaughtered. Of these, 500–700 were ethnic Chinese (Indonesia has a long history of anti-Chinese sentiment).

A few days after the assault on Dili, the Indonesian soldiers attacked other major towns and eventually pushed inland. On Christmas Day, the original 10,000 ABRI troops were supplemented by 15,000–20,000 more. By mid-February—a little over two months after the invasion began—60,000 East Timorese were dead.

After the invasion, Indonesia set up a puppet legislative assembly, whose 28 members—described by Indonesia as "prominent citizens of East Timor"—were handpicked by Indonesian intelligence officers, with the help of APODETI, who made sure they had no previous ties to FRETILIN or the UDT.

On May 31, 1976, this puppet assembly declared that East Timor wanted to become part of Indonesia. Observers at this event have stated that it was completely staged by the Indonesian authorities. The few journalists and junior diplomats from other countries who attended the proceedings were not permitted to speak with any delegates of the People's Assembly. As one journalist stated:

> Immediately after the council meeting, all were led back into their cars and briefly driven around the town before going straight back to the airport ....No one had a chance even to shake hands with council members, and executive members of the Provisional Government refused to answer press questions, climbing immediately into their new Volvo cars.

In July 1976, President Suharto signed into law East Timor's formal "integration" into the Unitary State of the Republic of Indonesia.

UN RESPONSE TO THE INVASION

Five days after the invasion, the United Nations General Assembly passed a resolution that deplored the invasion, called on Indonesia to withdraw immediately, and upheld the East Timorese people's right of self-determination. The vote was 72 to 10, with 43 abstentions, including the US, Canada and most Western European nations. Seven subsequent resolutions on East Timor have been passed by the General Assembly (the last one in 1982); France, Germany and Britain have abstained, and the US, Australia and Japan have voted *No* on most of them—even when the resolution was only to instruct the Secretary General to investigate the situation.

On December 22, 1975, at Portugal's urging, the UN Security Council unanimously passed a resolution that condemned Jakarta's invasion and occupation, and supported East Timor's right to self-determination. (A similar resolution passed in April 1976, with the US and Japan abstaining.)

José Ramos-Horta, FRETILIN's UN representative at the time, explained the vote this way: "Permanent members of the Security Council [couldn't] have abstained on such a blatant case of armed aggression involving a NATO ally [Portugal]," especially since "the Security Council is a more visible body than the General Assembly." In other words, the West's affirmative vote was more an attempt to save face than a condemnation of the invasion, and the earlier vote in the General Assembly more closely represented their position.

International legal specialist Roger Clark has argued that if further and stronger Security Council resolutions had been proposed, the US would have blocked their approval. A statement by Daniel Patrick Moynihan, US ambassador to the UN during the Ford administration, bears out Clark's analysis. Concerning UN inaction on East Timor, Moynihan boasted that "The [US] Department of State desired that the United Nations prove utterly ineffective in whatever measures it undertook. This task was given to me, and I carried it forward with no inconsiderable success."

A close look at individual countries' behind-the-scenes dealings with Indonesia shows that their behavior at the UN was part of a much larger pattern of support for Indonesia. Not only did a number of powerful Western or Western-aligned countries fail to condemn the invasion; they also either knew the invasion was imminent and did nothing to prevent it, or were actually complicit in Indonesia's brutality. The most significant accomplice was the US.

US SUPPORT FOR INDONESIA

America stands as it always has, against aggression, against those who would use force to replace the rule of law.

> US President George Bush, 1990,
> referring to the Iraqi invasion of Kuwait

When I think of Indonesia—a country on the equator with 180 million people, a median age of 18, and a Muslim ban on alcohol—I feel like I know what heaven looks like.

Coca-Cola President Donald R. Keough, c. 1992

It's clear that the US knew about the upcoming invasion and avoided taking any action that might have stopped it. In August 1975, Australia's ambassador to Indonesia cabled the Department of Foreign Affairs in Canberra (Australia's capital), as follows:

> The United States might have some influence on Indonesia at the present as Indonesia really wants and needs US assistance in its military re-equipment program.... But [US] Ambassador Newsom told me last night that he is under instructions from [US Secretary of State Henry] Kissinger personally not to involve himself in discussions on Timor with the Indonesians on the ground that the US is involved in enough problems of greater importance overseas at present....His present attitude is that the US should keep out of the Portuguese Timor situation and allow events to take their course.

US President Gerald Ford and Secretary of State Henry Kissinger were in Jakarta visiting Indonesian President Suharto the two days before the invasion. There's little doubt that Ford gave Suharto the green light to invade. Kissinger told reporters in Jakarta that "the US understands Indonesia's position on the question" of East Timor, and Ford said that, given a choice between East Timor and Indonesia, the US "had to be on the side of Indonesia." (US support for the invasion was important to Suharto because ABRI relied heavily on US weaponry—which US law states can only be used for defensive purposes.)

In early 1976, the US voiced its *de facto* recognition of Jakarta's annexation of East Timor. An unnamed US State Department official explained:

"In terms of the bilateral relations between the US and Indonesia, we are more or less condoning the incursion into East Timor."

These US actions weren't surprising, given the history of business relations between the two countries. By the end of World War I, the US and Japan supplied almost a third of the Dutch East Indies' imports. In turn, US-based corporations located there supplied the US with tin, rubber and oil. By 1939, the Dutch East Indies were supplying the US with over half of its needs for "no less than fifteen distinct commodities."

WWII radically changed the map of the Pacific, with the US emerging as the region's dominant power. US policymakers recognized that the region held great promise:

> These areas not only offer many markets for American products but are substantial producers of raw materials useful to our economy....Our merchant marine and commercial firms should be given the opportunity to take over a large portion of that trade formerly handled by the Japanese and their vessels.

George Kennan, Director of the Policy Planning Staff at the US State Department, noted that the US had "about 50% of the world's wealth but only 6.3% of its population," and offered this advice:

> Our real task in the coming period is to devise a pattern of relationships which will permit us to maintain this position of disparity without positive detriment to our national security. We should make a careful study to see what parts of the Pacific and Far Eastern world are absolutely vital to our security, and we should concentrate

our policy on seeing to it that those areas remain in hands which we can control or rely on.

Indonesia, with its fertile soils, wealth of natural resources and strategic location, is certainly an important area to "control or rely on." In a 1965 speech in Asia, Richard Nixon argued in favor of bombing North Vietnam to protect the "immense mineral potential" of Indonesia, which he later referred to as "by far the greatest prize in the southeast Asian area."

To protect its prizes, the US eventually killed over four million people in Vietnam, Cambodia and Laos between 1965 and 1975. In South Vietnam alone, the war resulted in a million widows and 879,000 orphans. It destroyed 9000 out of 15,000 hamlets, almost 40,000 square miles of farmland and 18,750 square miles of forest. Such carnage indicates what the US would be willing to support in Indonesia and East Timor.

In the late 1940s, US government and corporate leaders decided to support Indonesian independence over the continuing instability of Dutch rule (as mentioned above). To their chagrin, however, the new Indonesian government became highly nationalistic, anti-imperialist and non-aligned. Worried that the area might move beyond US control, Washington began (in the 1950s) to curry favor with the Indonesian army, through military assistance and training programs.

The US soon reaped the benefits of this policy. In 1965, using an alleged Communist plot to overthrow the government as an excuse, pro-US General Suharto assumed control of the military and launched "one of the great slaughters of our time." Hundreds of thousands of Indonesians were killed, mostly landless peasants and members of the Communist Party of Indonesia (many of whose names had been supplied to the army by the US Embassy in Jakarta).

Suharto's government repealed the previous regime's "extremely restrictive" investment laws and paved the way for large-scale foreign investment. By the 1970s, the US was investing more in Indonesia than in any other Southeast Asian country, even the Philippines. Part of that trade was arms—the State Department estimates that US companies supplied about 90% of the weapons used during the invasion of East Timor.

Indonesia's support for Western political objectives, liberal investment climate and repressive labor conditions—the minimum wage is less than $2 a day—make it very attractive to Western companies. Under Suharto, it developed into a major international business center. Extensive mining, logging and oil extraction take place there, as well as manufacturing by and for a wide variety of US companies, including Nike, Levi Strauss, Toys R Us, General Motors, Du Pont, Liz Claiborne and Tommy Hilfiger.

Support for Indonesia's actions in East Timor and elsewhere is a small price to pay for the investment opportunities and political support Indonesia offers. So the US not only refused to condemn the invasion, but sharply increased aid to Indonesia in its aftermath.

Weapons sales, already well established, were reduced during the year following the invasion. But when it looked as if Indonesia might run out of military equipment in 1977 (due to its activities in East Timor), the "human rights" administration of Jimmy Carter authorized sales of $112 million, up from $13 million the year before. Arms sales to Indonesia peaked at over $500 million from 1981 and 1986, during the Reagan administration.

Although Indonesia diversified its arms suppliers to include countries like Britain, France and Germany, in 1992–94 it was still importing 53% of its weapons from the US. And more than 2600 Indonesian military officers have been trained in the US since the invasion of East Timor, under a program called IMET (International Military Education and Training).

As a State Department official explained shortly after the invasion: "The United States wants to keep its relations with Indonesia close and friendly. [It's] a nation we do a lot of business with."

Because the corporate media tend to follow the lead of their governments, people in the West learned almost nothing about Indonesia's brutal invasion and the ensuing war. When political parties in East Timor were working toward independence from Portugal (in 1975), a number of US newspapers reported on the process. But after the invasion, news of East Timor largely disappeared from the Western press.

The *Los Angeles Times* is a typical example. From August 1975 till the December 7 invasion, it ran 16 articles dealing with East Timor. But from March 1976 to November 1979—at a time when Indonesia's occupation was described, in a report to the Australian parliament, as "indiscriminate killing on a scale unprecedented in post-World War

II history"—East Timor wasn't mentioned *once*. (For more on the occupation, see pp. 52–67.)

This neglect by the US media continued throughout the 1980s, but things began to improve after the Santa Cruz massacre in late 1991. The next year, in response to grassroots pressure—and in spite of strong opposition from the Bush administration and major US corporations—Congress cut off IMET funds worth $2.3 million. This was the first time Washington had refused aid to Indonesia since the invasion of East Timor.

When running for president in 1992, Bill Clinton called US policy toward East Timor "unconscionable," and his administration has indeed banned the sale of small and light arms, riot-control equipment, helicopter-mounted weaponry and armored personnel carriers to Indonesia. On the other hand, he's allowed the sale of hundreds of millions of dollars of other weaponry to Jakarta, and provided $500+ million in economic assistance from 1993 through 1998.

He side-stepped the IMET ban on by allowing Indonesia to purchase (rather than simply be given) the training, and used another Pentagon program, JCET (Joint Combined Exchange Training), to provide Kopassus (special forces troops responsible for many of the worst human rights violations in East Timor, including torture, extrajudicial executions and "disappearances") with training in sniper tactics, urban warfare, explosives, psychological operations and the like.

Even during the political crisis that led to Suharto's resignation in May 1998, the Clinton administration continued to back the regime.

Just ten hours before Suharto's resignation, Secretary of State Madeleine Albright was busy praising the dictator.

Congress was better. In 1998, the Senate unanimously passed a resolution that called on Clinton to work with the UN and US allies toward an internationally-supervised vote on self-determination for East Timor, and later in the year, both houses renewed a 1997 ban on US weapons in East Timor.

Although the US government's criminal partnership with Indonesia continues, it's increasingly limited and on shakier and shakier ground.

AUSTRALIAN SUPPORT FOR INDONESIA

It's important for Australia that the world understand that big countries cannot invade small neighbors and get away with it.

Australian Prime Minister Bob Hawke, 1990, referring to the Iraqi invasion of Kuwait

I don't see what you are getting excited about! The plain fact is that there are only 700,000 Timorese; what we are really concerned about is our relationship with 130,000,000 Indonesians.

An official of the Australian Foreign Affairs Department, circa the mid-1970s

Australia supported the first UN resolution condemning the invasion, with Prime Minister Fraser and his foreign minister both publicly rejecting Indonesia's absorption of East Timor. But that was largely due to massive popular opposition to the invasion.

Beneath the surface, a different story was unfolding. In January 1976, a month after the invasion, Australia's ambassador to Indonesia, Richard Woolcott, sent the following cable to Canberra:

> On the Timor issue...we face one of those broad foreign-policy decisions which face most countries at one timor [sic] or another. The Government is confronted by a choice between a moral stance, based on condemnation of Indonesia for the invasion of East Timor and on the assertion of the inalienable right of the people of East Timor to the right of self-determination, on the one hand, and a pragmatic and realistic acceptance of the longer-term inevitabilities of the situation on the other hand.
>
> It is a choice between what might be described as Wilsonian idealism or Kissingerian realism. The former is more proper and principled but the longer-term national interest may well be served by the latter. We do not think we can have it both ways.

From the actions that followed, Australia's choice is clear. Prime Minister Fraser attempted to undermine support for FRETILIN within Australia. He seized a radio transmitter in Darwin that had been used to communicate with FRETILIN inside East Timor, and later denied Australian entry visas to FRETILIN leaders in exile. In addition, he reportedly gave an informal OK to Indonesia's takeover of East Timor during a visit with Suharto in Jakarta in October 1976.

Australian military assistance to Jakarta nearly doubled between 1975 and 1981—when the bulk of Indonesia's killings in East Timor took place.

US pressure may have had an influence on Australia's stance. It's been reported that high-ranking members of the Ford administration warned Fraser to back down from his criticisms of Indonesia's takeover of East Timor. Given US influence over Australia, it seems likely that Australia would have complied. As a 1974 Australian Defense Department paper noted, "It is desirable...that Australian policy...pay regard to US interests and reactions, as an important ally and principal power in the Western strategic community."

Still, as with other Western powers, Australia's reasons for acquiescing to the invasion were largely economic. When Gough Whitlam became prime minister in 1972, he made it clear that Indonesia was the key to establishing stronger trade and investment connections with the Association of South East Asian Nations (ASEAN). Whitlam then stated, "It goes without saying that the number one [foreign policy] goal of my government is to strengthen relations with Indonesia."

One reason for that is the Timor Gap, an area of continental shelf in the Timor Sea (which separates Australia and East Timor). The waters of the Timor Gap lie over one of the richest deposits of oil and natural gas in the world. As Ambassador Woolcott wrote in August 1975:

> We are all aware of the Australian defense interest in the Portuguese Timor situation but I wonder whether the Department has ascertained the interest of the Minister of the Department of Minerals and Energy in the Timor situation....
> The present gap in the agreed sea border...could be much more readily negotiated with

> Indonesia...than with Portugal or an indepen-
> dent Portuguese Timor.
>   I know I am recommending a pragmatic
> rather than a principled stand but that is what
> national interest and foreign policy is all about.

In January 1978, Australia became the only Western country ever to officially recognize Indonesia's sovereignty over East Timor; with that out of the way, the two countries entered into negotiations over the Timor Gap.

In December 1989, on a plane flying over the Timor Sea, Australia's and Indonesia's foreign ministers signed the Timor Gap Treaty, which sets out boundaries for oil and gas exploration in the seabed. (This treaty is almost certainly illegal, since international law prohibits recognition of sovereignty over territory acquired by illegitimate force.)

Exploratory drilling has been taking place for a number of years, and oil began being pumped in 1998. A number of major oil companies, such as British Petroleum, Australia-based BHP and US-based Marathon Petroleum, are involved.

Today, Australia engages in joint military maneuvers and exchanges military intelligence with Indonesia, and supplies military hardware (like naval patrol boats) and training to ABRI. In 1995, Prime Minister Paul Keating signed a security agreement with the Suharto regime, helping to bring the Australian military closer to ABRI.

No Western country has done more to accommodate Indonesia diplomatically than Australia. In 1993, it went so far as to urge Washington and London to soften their criticisms of Jakarta's human rights record. And in early 1998, in the midst of Indonesia's economic crisis, the new government of Prime Minister John Howard asked the International Monetary Fund to show the Suharto regime greater flexibility.

INDONESIA'S OTHER SUPPORTERS

Five months before the invasion, President Suharto visited Prime Minister Pierre Trudeau in Canada. One of the four items for discussion was "Prospects and Developments in Portuguese Timor." The meeting went well for Suharto—Canada pledged an additional CDN$200 million in aid. Several attempts to discover the nature of the discussions (by means of Access to Information requests) have been unsuccessful, but Canada's behavior following the invasion—under both Liberal and Conservative governments—provides some clues.

Canada abstained from voting on the first five UN General Assembly resolutions on East Timor, and voted *No* on the last three. Indonesia has consistently been among the top recipients of Canada's direct, country-to-country aid, receiving CDN$35 million in 1996–97.

Canadian investments in Indonesia are estimated at CDN$8 billion, primarily in mining, oil, gas and infrastructure development. Inco Ltd.'s vast nickel-mining operation in Sulawesi leads the way. Drawn by cheap labor and lax environmental regulations, Inco has been expanding in Indonesia while laying off workers at home.

Canada has sold weapons to Indonesia—both directly and through sales to US arms companies who sell to Indonesia—and many of those weapons have been used in East Timor. Arms sales, halted in 1992, resumed under Prime Minister Jean Chrétien in 1993, whose government has identified Indonesia as a prime trade target.

From 1993 to 1997, Canada issued permits valued at CDN$420 million for arms exports (almost exclusively spare parts) to Indonesia. It's now one of Canada's largest export markets in Southeast Asia, with two-way trade of about CDN$1.6 billion in 1997.

In November 1994, Chrétien signed a nuclear cooperation agreement with Indonesia, the first step toward providing it with Canadian nuclear reactor technology. This is alarming, since other countries have in the past used such technology to help develop nuclear weapons.

Japan voted against all eight UN General Assembly resolutions on East Timor. Its cozy relationship to the Suharto government can only be understood in light of the fact that it was the second largest foreign investor in Indonesia in 1975 (and now is the largest). According to an IMF report, Japan received 37% of Indonesia's exports in 1991 (predominately oil and natural gas) and provided Indonesia with 25% of its imports.

Japan gives the bulk of all the direct, country-to-country aid Indonesia gets. In 1996, Japan's contribution amounted to $965 million, making Indonesia its top foreign aid recipient—even though Japanese law requires the government to consider democratization and basic human rights and freedoms when granting foreign aid.

A diplomatic white paper from the Japanese government makes it quite clear how important Indonesia has become to Japan's future:

Indonesia has a strong, mutually dependent relation with Japan through provision of oil and natural gas and acceptance of direct investment. And Indonesia is a very important country for Japan because it is located in an area with important international sea routes and because it has a large political influence in Southeast Asia.

East Timor—a tiny half-island with relatively few resources—can scarcely compete with what Indonesia has to offer.

In July 1975, when the Indonesians were in the early stages of Operation Komodo, the British ambassador to Indonesia wrote to the Foreign Office that "the people of Portuguese Timor are in no condition to exercise their right to self-determination." But he added that it would be best not to acknowledge this openly:

Certainly as seen from here it is in Britain's interest that Indonesia should absorb the territory as soon as and as unobtrusively as possible; and that if it comes to the crunch and there is a row in the United Nations, we should keep our heads down and avoid siding against the Indonesian government.

Britain abstained from all eight votes on East Timor in the UN General Assembly, and continues to sell arms to Indonesia. In 1978, the British government licensed the sale of eight British-made Hawk ground attack jets, which ABRI used in its saturation bombing during the encirclement and annihilation campaign (for more about that, see pp. 52–67).

In 1993, the British government approved the sale of 24 more Hawk aircraft to Jakarta; in 1996, they approved the sale of an additional 16. Although Tony Blair came to power in 1997 promising an "ethical foreign policy," his Labour government is proceeding with the sale of the Hawks, and has approved at least 22 new arms export licenses for Indonesia.

In addition to being one of Indonesia's top weapons suppliers, Britain is now its second largest foreign investor (after Japan), having poured in over $30 billion since 1967.

From 1967 through 1991, billions of dollars in grants and bank credits were supplied to the genocidal Suharto regime by the Inter-Governmental Group on Indonesia (IGGI)—a consortium of donor countries that includes Japan, the US, France, Britain, the Netherlands and Germany (the last two are also major arms suppliers to Indonesia).

Following the Santa Cruz massacre, some donor countries tried to link aid to human rights. In response, Suharto disbanded the IGGI in early 1992 and set in its place something called the Consultative Group on Indonesia (CGI), chaired by the World Bank. At its July 1998 meeting in Paris, CGI members pledged $7.9 billion in aid to Jakarta.

As of 1997, Indonesia's external debt totaled almost $138 billion, leading the World Bank to characterize it as "a severely indebted middle income country." Since then, Indonesia's economy has collapsed, and its foreign debt has surely increased significantly.

INDONESIA'S WAR OF OCCUPATION

We are dying as a people and as a nation.
Carlos Belo, Bishop of Dili, 1989

In the first few months after the invasion began, Indonesia's army (ABRI) could only capture major towns and villages and a few transportation corridors, despite heavy naval and aerial bombardment. In the rural areas, where the vast majority of the population lived, ABRI progressed at "a snail's pace" (in the words of the US Defense Intelligence Agency).

ABRI also suffered heavy casualties at the hands of FALINTIL (FRETILIN's army). Australian intelligence analysts estimated that there were more than 450 Indonesian military casualties in the first few weeks, and in the first four months of 1976, as many as 2000 Indonesian troops were killed.

This was largely because FRETILIN had expected the invasion for months. Well before December 1975, it had begun to establish bases and relocate its forces in the country's interior. With 2500 former full-time Portuguese troops, 7000 part-time militia, 10,000 reservists—plus civilians who had received military training following the civil war with the UDT—FALINTIL had a formidable contingent of fighters. In addition, it had a detailed knowledge of East Timor's geography and large supplies of weapons left by the Portuguese.

As a result, FRETILIN was able to maintain effective control over the majority of East Timorese territory for many months. Within the liberated areas, life continued as usual—schools and agricultural cooperatives continued to function, and FRETILIN radio continued to broadcast throughout the territory.

But beginning in September 1977, things took a turn for the worse. ABRI's plan was to push the resistance into the center of the country, where the fighters could be killed or captured, and to force the rural population to the coastal lowlands, where they could be more easily controlled. (Catholic sources called this "encirclement and annihilation.")

Using tens of thousands of ground troops and counterinsurgency aircraft called Broncos (newly acquired from the US, they were ideally suited for the rugged terrain of East Timor), ABRI forces began penetrating the interior of the island. Along the way, they bombed forested areas to defoliate ground cover and used chemical sprays to destroy crops and livestock.

Lourenço, a former UDT supporter who later began working with FRETILIN, described the annihilation of a section of FALINTIL's eastern zone:

> I was in Matebian [near Baguia], where it's all mountain and rocks....On 17 October 1978 some Indonesians got right to the bottom of Matebian mountain and that's when we started to fight back. For those first two months, October and November, we were very successful and about 3000 Indonesians died. Then they got angry and scared to come close and started to bomb us from the air.

They bombed twice a day, in the morning and afternoon, with four black planes. Their name I know now is Broncos, but we called them *scorpions* because they had a tail that curves up at the back like that insect. Their bombs left a big hole about two meters deep.

Then they got new supersonic planes. Our people were very frightened of those because you didn't even hear they were there until they were gone. Those supersonics would zoom along the valley so fast we couldn't shoot them....

We knew by radio from the south zone that the Indonesians had dropped four napalm bombs there. Then they dropped two of these on us. I saw all the flames and heard people shouting and screaming. I was on another mountain but I could see well....By foot it took half an hour to go down and up again, and by the time we got there everything was completely burnt.

We saw a whole area about fifty meters square all burnt, no grass, nothing except ash. On the rocks it was a brown reddish color and on the ground ash too, not ordinary grey ash, a sort of yellow ash, like beach sand. You couldn't see where bodies had been. There was nothing except ash and burnt rocks on the whole area, but we had heard those people screaming.

Additional Western military sales, including US F-5 jets and A-4 bombers and British Hawk ground attack aircraft, greatly increased ABRI's destructive capacity. With such attacks repeated over and over, FALINTIL had little chance of beating back the Indonesians, and many units had to surrender. Xavier, a guerrilla fighter, describes his capture by ABRI:

In 1979 all our people, nearly 3000 from my Laclo area, were caught by the Indonesians near the main coast road where you pass to Manatutu and Baucau. We go to the highest point and stayed there for a month trying every way to get out.

The Indonesians attacked us from the beach and from Manatutu, Dili and Baucau. All came together and surrounded us. Some fighters escaped and took guns back to other FALINTIL. I was captured because I was responsible—that was my position. I had to stay with my people— I couldn't leave. They captured me without my gun or I would be dead.

We were interrogated, but we spoke no Bahasa Indonesia, so a Timorese interpreted. He said, "Don't be afraid, always say something, say anything." The interpreter made up our answers. He was Timorese too, he tried to protect us.

There were so many people to interrogate and we were all telling wrong things anyway. But when they took us to Dili, slowly they wiped out nearly all of us who'd been fighters. Spies and informers had time to do their work there.

By the time the encirclement and annihilation campaign ended in March 1979, "many thousands" of civilians and many top FRETILIN leaders were dead; others were captured or had surrendered. FALINTIL lost 80% of its troops and more than 90% of its weapons, and its internal and international lines of communication were completely severed. The captured troops, and the tens of thousands of civilians who fled from the mountains, were either relocated in "guarded camps" or deported to the offshore island of Atauro.

Its forces and weaponry devastated, FALINTIL was nonetheless able to regroup and reorganize— a pattern that was to be repeated several times in the next decade. Under the leadership of Xanana Gusmão, a local commander in the east, FALINTIL reorganized its forces into small, relatively independent units throughout the country.

The change in strategy and organization allowed it to mount more attacks on ABRI in 1980 than during the eighteen-month encirclement and annihilation campaign. Although FALINTIL couldn't reestablish control over any population centers, it was able to build a covert support network within Indonesian-controlled villages and to regain control of significant amounts of rural territory. ABRI casualties mounted and morale declined.

By March 1981 FRETILIN had established enough communication among its units to hold a national conference. There Xanana was elected head of FRETILIN and commander-in-chief.

In response to FRETILIN's resurgence, ABRI launched a new operation in mid-1981 that included something called a "fence of legs." About 80,000 East Timorese males, ranging in age from 8 to 50, were forced to walk in a line across the countryside in front of ABRI troops, protecting them from attack by FALINTIL guerrillas. The objective was to either flush out the guerrillas or to force them into the center of the island where they could be massacred. A participant, Cristiano da Costa, describes what it was like in one of many areas after the campaign:

> It started from all parts of East Timor, all driving towards Aitana, near Lakluta, that was to be the middle of the circle. The front line was Timorese forced to take part. When the circle was small

enough, the army bombarded the area, then soldiers went to finish off any people left there.

One week later I was forced to go up with a
group of soldiers to do a final clean-up....We
smelt the bodies before we found them. The
heads had been cut off the first bodies, one
woman and four men....The heads were on the
other bodies I saw.

We found three other men tied by the feet
hanging upside down in trees... another two
men were tied with their hands behind the
trunks of trees. Their faces looked beaten and it
looked like knife wounds to their stomachs.

On the ground beside them there were six
others, two women and two children and an old
man and an old woman....There was dried
blood on those bodies....The smell was very bad
and the flies....It was not possible to identify
those people; if they were my own brother or
sister I could not know them.

Given only the most meager of provisions by
the Indonesian military, many of the walkers in
the "fence of legs" campaign starved to death. The
operation also greatly disrupted agricultural production, leading to severe food shortages in most
regions of the country.

While many FRETILIN groups surrendered or
were slaughtered during the campaign, many
evaded capture. By late 1982, FRETILIN had
again reorganized and was launching a number of
attacks all over the country (including one on
Dili), putting local Indonesian military leaders
increasingly on the defensive.

A number of the officials decided to negotiate
cease-fire agreements with FRETILIN, culminating in a country-wide cease-fire agreement on

March 23, 1983. (ABRI and the Indonesian government hoped to keep the cease-fire secret and were greatly embarrassed when the news broke internationally.)

Within five months, however, ABRI Commander-in-Chief Benny Murdani unilaterally broke the cease-fire, declaring, "This time no fooling around. We are going to hit them without mercy." On August 17, 1983, Indonesia launched a new campaign.

But since FRETILIN had taken advantage of the cease-fire to consolidate its underground network in the resettlement villages, it could resist fiercely—even though it faced massive numbers of ABRI troops, as well as bombing from the air and sea. Once again, ABRI wasn't able to make any significant gains, and withdrew its troops to the major roads and population centers at the end of 1984.

During the latter half of the 1980s, ABRI launched a number of offensives, hoping to capture Xanana Gusmão, and it continued to use "fence of legs" operations. But, in large part, the military situation remains stalemated.

Between 20,000 and 30,000 ABRI troops control the main towns and other strategic locations, while about 600 FALINTIL guerrilla fighters are spread out in small groups throughout the countryside. ABRI still launches offensives from time to time, resulting in occasional clashes with FALINTIL.

The reason many of Indonesia's troops are concentrated in the towns is to contain potential political unrest among East Timorese youth, who are almost universally in favor of independence. This strategy paid off in November 1992, when ABRI soldiers captured Xanana Gusmão hiding in a safe house in Dili. Today, FALINTIL is led by Tuar Matan Ruak.

YOU'RE INDONESIANS, DAMN IT!

Indonesia's efforts to gain military control of East Timor have been the most violent and visible part of the occupation. But to achieve its long-term goal of "Indonesianizing" East Timor, it has used other, sometimes more insidious, forms of control against the civilian population.

Indonesianization is an ongoing process with a missionary and racist zeal. As a former Indonesian military commander described the task: "It is the new Indonesian civilization we are bringing. And it is not easy to civilize backward people."

The first step in this civilizing mission is physical control of the population. As early as April 1976, FRETILIN's underground radio network reported the existence of "guarded camps" in Indonesian-controlled areas. According to a July 1979 report by the Australian Council for Overseas Aid, there were fifteen camps with a population of 318,921 "displaced persons":

> [ABRI] ordered people to move from their own village or district into one or other of the fifteen centers as part of its strategy against FRETILIN. The strategy, which resembles counter-insurgency techniques employed against guerrillas in places such as Rhodesia, Malaysia and Vietnam, has increased the

Indonesian army's control over the local population and allowed it, in the words of an
Indonesian parliamentarian, "to separate the
people from the terrorists" (i.e., FRETILIN).

The forced relocation, combined with ABRI's
brutal military campaign, disrupted local farming
and resulted in widespread famine. In one camp,
where 80% of its 8,000 inhabitants suffered from
malnutrition, a visiting delegate from the International Committee of the Red Cross called the situation "as bad as Biafra and potentially as serious
as Kampuchea [Cambodia]" Forced labor, including carrying ammunition and supplies into combat
areas, was also common.

A lot of the people in the camps were soon
moved to "resettlement villages," many of which
still exist today. They're located far away from
the FALINTIL resistance, usually near asphalt
roads to make them easily accessible to ABRI.
When settling the camps, the occupation authorities deliberately broke up the traditional forms
of social organization, placing people from the
same villages, clans or hamlets in different resettlement villages, so that an organized resistance
would be less likely to develop.

Within the villages and towns, the military,
police and *babinsas* (the eyes and ears of ABRI
who are present in each neighborhood or vil-
lage) have kept a tight rein on the people.
According to the former bishop of Dili, "The
babinsas are everywhere. They are the ones
who have to know about everything happening
in the villages and the settlements. Everything
has to be reported to them."

Justino, a visitor to the villages, describes the physical control and deplorable conditions found there:

There were many resettlement villages—we call them concentration camps. There were fifty camps around Baucau in 1979. People were brought to a camp a long way from their own place. They missed their land and their belongings, their ancestors and *lulik* [sacred] things. The camps were for the Indonesian military to control people and keep them away from Resistance fighters....

The camps were open areas, no fences, with small Timorese houses made of bamboo that last a few months—people built them themselves. To get into a camp you had to get special permission. I visited sometimes with a priest.

I didn't talk much to [the people in the camps] because there were informers and the military were always there, but I saw a lot of sick and starving people and I know many died because they weren't allowed to move far. They couldn't farm or collect enough food. If they went far outside the camp, they were suspected of contacting guerrillas and could be shot or put in prison or disappear.

A second step in Indonesianization is control of the economy. Soon after the invasion, Indonesian interests simply took over former Portuguese colonial enterprises. Indonesian authorities also began to take lands traditionally held by groups of hamlets (maintaining that no one owns traditionally-held lands, since there aren't any formal tenants) and to give them to local officials or pro-Indonesian native rulers.

Then, beginning in 1991, the Indonesian authorities requested that all private property owners convert their property certificates from the Portuguese to the Indonesian system. Since there's been massive dislocation from the war, and since Indonesia requires that land be "owner-occupied," this new system threatens both private landholdings by East Timorese living in exile abroad and traditionally-held lands, and will further concentrate land in the hands of Indonesian interests.

But even those who still work their land face great economic hardship. Until the early 1990s, for example, farmers who grew coffee were forced to sell it to P.T. Denok, a military monopoly set up by General Benny Murdani and a few associates immediately after the invasion. As an Indonesian military commander in East Timor remarked, it was "the only company that landed with the marines. They came together."

P.T. Denok's monopoly resulted in declining incomes for small East Timorese farmers, while the company's coffee profits have allowed it to diversify. One of its subsidiaries, P. T. Scent, has a monopoly on the collection and sale of sandalwood, which have increased significantly under the Indonesian occupation.

Today the military-affiliated P.T. Batara Indra Group controls P.T. Denok, P.T. Scent and a number of other subsidiaries in East Timor. The group owns Dili's only movie theater and its two best hotels, is involved in marble production, and imports a wide variety of consumer products.

In 1994, a leading Indonesian academic characterized the group's control of the East Timorese economy as a virtual monopoly. For reasons that are unclear, Denok's power seems to have declined significantly over the last few years.

Outside the military-controlled areas of the economy, Indonesian business interests almost completely dominate East Timorese commerce. Indonesian entrepreneurs have filled the economic vacuum created by the slaughter and flight of most East Timor's ethnic Chinese. Basic industries that produced agricultural tools, clothing, household goods and building materials during the Portuguese era have largely disappeared, and these goods are now imported from Indonesia. A 1980 Indonesian anthropological study warned:

> There needs to be some form of protection given to prevent big business commoditizing land and commercializing everyday life in the more remote areas. Without protection the East Timorese will simply become victims of moneyed interests from other regions [of Indonesia].

A 1990 follow-up study stated that the fear that the East Timorese subsistence economy will be "marginalized by capitalists and 'foreign' [i.e. Indonesian] entrepreneurs is well founded."

A third step of Indonesianization is control of the educational system, which completely neglects any information about East Timor that doesn't correspond to Jakarta's official viewpoint. Indonesian (called Bahasa Indonesia) is the only language allowed in schools. Military culture is also taught, and all students must memorize *Pancasila,* the supposed ideological basis of Indonesian society.

The school system also strongly encourages physical education (which is closely connected to the militarization of society) and membership in *Pramuka,* the state-controlled scout organization. Said one refugee, "There is a lot of physical education, less academic work and considerable singing of songs—the Indonesian anthem, the *Pancasila* set to music which you must memorize, school songs and songs patriotic to Indonesia."

But while Indonesia asserts that the number of schools in East Timor has increased dramatically since the invasion, illiteracy remains high. This is probably due as much to East Timorese resistance to Indonesianization as it is to Jakarta's misplaced educational priorities.

Not trusting that all these tactics will sufficiently Indonesianize the local population, Jakarta has resorted to other, more severe measures. They've begun a World Bank-funded program to decrease the birth rate of East Timorese women. A 1986 letter from inside East Timor describes the coercive nature of this program:

> Officials of the state planning program are present in every little village and hamlet to make people limit their number of children, and each family is only allowed to have three children. In the interior the military force our women to receive injections, and pills are being distributed to them for the same effect. All the women are being forced to take part in this. It is one way the enemy has to make our ethnic identity disappear.

International human rights groups and many East Timorese have accused Jakarta's family planning program of sterilizing East Timorese women without their knowledge, especially in the aftermath of the encirclement and annihilation campaign. Whether this is true or not, Jakarta's motives in attempting to lower the birth rate are certainly highly suspect. As the bishop of Dili, Carlos Belo, points out, "With so many dead, we have no population problem here."

While attempting to limit the East Timorese population, Indonesian authorities actively encourage Indonesians from throughout the country to migrate to East Timor. Under the guise of relieving population pressures in the relatively crowded islands like Java and Bali, and filling "empty" land in places like East Timor, Jakarta uses this "transmigration" program to try to create a pan-Indonesian identity and to serve the security needs of the military.

Land given to the transmigrants was either formerly owned by East Timorese who were forcibly relocated, or is deemed "underutilized" by the Indonesian authorities. In neither situation are the former owners compensated.

Through its "transmigration" program, the Suharto government resettled 662 Indonesian families (2,808 people) in East Timor through 1993. Indonesia continues to develop new transmigration sites throughout East Timor, especially in areas with fertile soils, or where guerrilla activity is high.

Far more significant than the relatively small number of transmigrants are the so-called "voluntary" or "spontaneous" migrants. Jakarta gives them the legal licenses needed to relocate within Indonesia, and often provides them with resources like land. Jakarta also draws people to East Timor by offering jobs in areas like education and administration.

While there are no precise figures, most observers estimate that there are at least 150,000 Indonesian settlers in East Timor, out of a total population of about 800,000–900,000. This heavy influx of Indonesian migrants, businesspeople and capital has marginalized the indigenous population economically.

Another thrust of Indonesianization is Jakarta's attempt to make its invasion of East Timor look like a civil war between East Timorese in favor of integration with Indonesia and those opposed to it. Two ABRI battalions of East Timorese have been formed, mostly made up of conscripts. ABRI has also formed local militias, often with compulsory participation.

"Jorge," now a refugee in Australia, describes his experience in one such militia:

> I was in high school, a student, when the war started in Timor. I had no political ties, didn't belong to any party.
>
> My friends and I were forced to join the Indonesian army. We were warned; all who didn't join the army had to take the consequences. That means that they say you are communist.
>
> None of us wanted to but there was no way not to fight. If you don't fight, you get killed yourself.
>
> I went on operations to kill other Timorese, ordinary people. Then I felt strange. None of us felt good. At first we are sad, we have remorse,

but after two or three years, it was easy. You get used to killing....

I was forced to kill my best friend. I don't want to talk about it. I don't feel good when I think about it....They knew he was my friend and I was forced to shoot him. They do these things to test you.

DEVELOPMENTS SINCE SANTA CRUZ AND FUTURE PROSPECTS

The concept of realpolitik [is] the denial of the individual conscience, the death of the conscience of a people.

Xanana Gusmão, Defense Plea, May 17, 1993

Until the Santa Cruz massacre in November 1991, the East Timor conflict seemed to be a forgotten war. Since then, however, East Timor's international allies have increased significantly. There are now active solidarity groups in many places, including the Philippines, Japan, Malaysia, Thailand, Brazil and almost all the Western countries.

Certain governments have also been playing a very supportive role—Ireland, for example, and African countries that were formerly Portuguese colonies, like Angola and Mozambique. Portugal itself, motivated by strong public sentiment and national embarrassment over its abandonment of its former colonial subjects, has greatly intensified its efforts to defend the rights of the East Timorese.

Support for East Timor has also grown greatly in the legislatures of several powerful countries, most importantly the United States and Britain. And several establishment publications, like *The New York Times* and *The Economist,* have called upon Indonesia to withdraw from East Timor, and to respect its right to decide its own destiny.

Backing for East Timorese self-determination has also increased within Indonesia itself. Many major prodemocracy figures, including Amien Rais, head of the National Trust Party; Budiman Sujatmiko, the jailed leader of the People's Democratic Party; and labor leader Muchtar Pakpahan have demanded that Jakarta allow East Timor to hold free elections on independence.

Within East Timor, mass public protest resurfaced in November 1994, when 29 East Timorese students and workers occupied the US embassy in Jakarta during President Clinton's visit to the Asia-Pacific Economic Conference (APEC) summit. Demonstrations and riots erupted in Dili and other towns, with protesters sometimes targeting Indonesian settlers and businesses.

Sporadic anti-occupation protests continued in APEC's aftermath. At the same time, international attention on—and activism around—East Timor continued to grow, culminating in the awarding of the 1996 Nobel Peace Prize to José Ramos-Horta, chief diplomat of the East Timorese resistance, and Bishop Carlos Belo, head of East Timor's Catholic Church.

(As the only public institution in East Timor that has survived the Indonesian occupation, the Church serves as a psychological and spiritual refuge for the East Timorese, over 90% of whom are Catholic. Under the leadership of Bishop Belo, the Church has become an outspoken defender of human rights in East Timor, often incurring the deep suspicion and ire of Indonesian authorities.)

A new umbrella organization now represents FRETILIN, the UDT and all East Timorese groups worldwide that are dedicated to national self-determination. Called the CNRT (National Council of Timorese Resistance), it was formed at a convention in April 1998. Xanana Gusmão was elected president of the CNRT's political and executive councils. (He continues to lead the resistance from detention in Jakarta, where he's serving a 20-year sentence for "rebellion.")

The fall of Suharto in May 1998 provided new opportunities for East Timor. Facing political instability, economic collapse and intense international scrutiny, the government of Habibie (Suharto's hand-picked successor) made an offer of "special autonomy" for East Timor in June 1998. Under the plan, East Timor would run many of its internal affairs, but remain part of Indonesia.

Mass demonstrations quickly made it clear that the vast majority of East Timorese rejected the plan and demanded their right to self-determination. At the same time, elements of the Indonesian military showed their opposition even to "special autonomy" by organizing Indonesian settlers and East Timorese (many forcibly) into "civilian militias." Armed by the military, these groups have terrorized the East Timorese population, killing scores of defenseless civilians.

In contrast, Jakarta's diplomats have been showing unprecedented flexibility. In January 1999, Habibie declared that he would grant independence to East Timor if its people rejected the autonomy offer, and Indonesia has even signed an accord with Portugal (still legally the administering power of East Timor) for a popular vote on autonomy in East Timor. This election, to be conducted by the United Nations, is scheduled for late August, 1999.

But the Indonesian military knows that a free vote will overwhelmingly reject Indonesia's rule, so the paramilitary terror continues. The message is clear: refusing to remain part of Indonesia will mean hell on earth for the East Timorese.

Unless the UN's ruling powers, particularly the United States, put significant pressure on the Indonesian military, it's difficult to see how the process can go forward. But regardless of what happens in the short-term, East Timor's struggle for freedom will continue.

As their resistance has demonstrated so dramatically through the years, the will of the East Timorese people for independence is undying. As Xanana Gusmão once said, "To resist is to win." Through its resistance to the Indonesian military's tyranny, East Timor survives.

Those of us who live outside East Timor can help the long-suffering East Timorese not only to survive but to live. Strong public pressure on the US and other Western countries, as well as support for Indonesia's democracy, labor and human rights movements, can force Indonesia to withdraw and ensure that the East Timorese realize their right to self-determination.

MY VISITS TO €AST TIMOR

The will of the people shall be the basis of the authority of government.

Article 21(3) of the *Universal Declaration of Human Rights,* adopted by the UN General Assembly, December 10, 1948

East Timor has been open to foreign tourists since 1989, but few researchers or journalists were allowed entry in the months following the Santa Cruz massacre. So when I first went there in July 1992, I called myself a tourist.

My flight from West Timor to Dili gave me my first glimpse of the half-island. Dominated by mountains, East Timor's terrain is quite rugged, but it's also quite beautiful.

As my flight approached Dili's airport, the rural landscape gave way to a medium-sized, Mediterranean-looking town, nestled around a natural harbor. With a population of about 120,000, Dili is East Timor's largest town. Since it suffered extensive bombing in World War II and because it has grown tremendously since 1975, many of the buildings are fairly new, but much of the architecture still bears the stamp of the Portuguese colonial past.

The first day, I tried to get my bearings. Walking around Dili, I got a sense of the diverse origins of the East Timorese, who speak a number of indigenous languages. Tetum serves as the lingua franca and is spoken and understood in most parts of the country. Indonesian and—to a far lesser extent—Portuguese are also spoken.

It didn't take long to sense the resentment and fear that permeate East Timorese life. In Indonesia itself, the streets are full of bustling activity, and a foreigner hears the ubiquitous greeting "Hello, mister" from young faces. In Dili, the streets are more deserted, and when I passed people, many seemed afraid even to say hello.

On my first day, I stopped a young man on the street for directions to the nearest restaurant. I asked him how things were in Dili. His vague, hushed reply—that there were many problems—warned me not press further.

His fear wasn't hard to understand. There are dozens of military installations throughout Dili and truckloads of Indonesian soldiers frequently drive through the streets. Less obvious, but even more pernicious, is the extensive network of spies—and paid or coerced informants, often East Timorese—that permeates the city.

A Catholic priest in Dili told me he feared spies in his own congregation. In central East Timor, a seminarian described his country as "a prison" in which "we are slaves of the Indonesians." In Baucau, a young man darted out of the bushes near my hotel to give me a letter for the International Committee of the Red Cross.

And in a nearby town, a nun whom I'll call Sister Maria told me the story of Rosa, a girl enrolled in a local Catholic school. The nuns were having great difficulty getting Rosa to accept the Christian concept of forgiveness. Rosa finally told them why.

Several years ago, Indonesian soldiers came to Rosa's home and took away her older brother, accusing him of having ties to the armed resistance. Too afraid to inquire, the family had no idea where the army had taken him or if he was even alive. Two days later, soldiers returned to Rosa's home with a bag. Inside it was her brother's head.

Understandably, stories like these frightened me—and with good reason. On a number of occasions I was followed, and there were many times when a "friend" would ask far too many questions of me. The photographer who had met my plane and snapped pictures of all deplaning passengers subsequently appeared at a number of restaurants where I was eating.

I later learned that he met all planes or ferries arriving from West Timor or other islands. Twice he came to my hotel, pretending to socialize with the proprietors.

As time passed, I began attracting increasing attention from Indonesian intelligence. In one town, someone from military intelligence came looking for me only 30 minutes after I arrived. I spent the next hour with the English-speaking district military commander who politely, but persistently, questioned me about my intentions in East Timor, wanting to know if I was a journalist. (He'd learned English while being trained at Fort Benning, Georgia.) One night, someone stood outside my low-budget hotel room window for a couple of hours, peering at me in bed through a little hole in the window.

Although such experiences left me almost constantly fearful, my anxiety paled in comparison to the constant fear that permeates everyday life in East Timor. It would be difficult, if not impossible, to find an East Timorese who has not lost a family member or a close friend to the Indonesian military.

When I returned to East Timor more than four years later, I saw evidence of change as soon as my taxi left the airport: On a wall near the airport entrance, someone had boldly spraypainted "Viva Bishop Belo," a tribute to the recently-announced Nobel Peace Prize winner.

During my 1992 visit, most East Timorese seemed too afraid to even make direct eye contact with me. This time, many people greeted me as I walked the streets in Dili. Some, particularly younger people, flashed me the V-for-victory sign, a display of their nationalist sympathies.

Despite these openings, East Timor was still a place where few people dared to speak their minds in public. "We are very happy that the world has recognized our suffering with the Nobel Prize," a middle-aged woman told me in a brief conversation on a shady street, "but we still live in a prison." Our talk ended abruptly when a stranger appeared.

The streets of Dili were empty by 9 pm. According to several people I interviewed, Indonesian soldiers randomly attack people, especially youths, who are outside at night.

Matters are worse in rural areas, where the Catholic Church has less of a presence. "Outside the towns, people are at the total mercy of the Indonesian military," one priest said.

In most places I visited, there was also evidence of the resilient, defiant spirit that's fueled more than two decades of a national resistance movement. A small but vibrant guerrilla army and a very large, extensive, and effective underground are active in towns and villages throughout the country.

I saw this firsthand when I spent 24 hours with David Alex and ten of the 150 FALINTIL guerrillas under his command. A 21-year veteran in the struggle against ABRI, Alex was, at the time, third in the FALINTIL command.

Underground activists drove me to a rural safe house, where I was taken on a lengthy hike to the guerrillas' mountain camp. My transport in and out of the area relied on the cooperation of numerous people from many walks of life, exposing the hollowness of Indonesia's claims that the resistance is marginalized and isolated within East Timor.

(ABRI soldiers captured David Alex in June 1997. He died shortly thereafter in Indonesian custody, under very suspicious circumstances.)

Throughout my visits to East Timor in 1992, 1996 and 1998, it was obvious everywhere I went that Indonesia has failed miserably to win the hearts and minds of the East Timorese. As a prominent resistance figure said to me in 1992, "Politically, we've won. However, it is a question of force—something we don't have."

Over the last few years, however, East Timor's strength has increased considerably. As the resistance within East Timor, support within Indonesia and international solidarity continue to grow, it now seems likely that the people of East Timor will realize their human right to self-determination in the foreseeable future.

It will certainly be difficult, but we can all help in this process. Our common humanity demands no less.

WHAT YOU CAN DO

In this brutal world, there are many causes worth putting your time, effort and money into. But there's probably nothing you can do that will save more lives per dollar, or hour, you invest than to support one of the East Timor solidarity group listed below: *Arthur Naiman*

East Timor Action Network (ETAN/US) • PO Box 1182, White Plains NY 10602 • 914 428 7299 • fax: 914 428 7383 • email: *etan-us@igc.apc.org* • This is also the UN Office for the International Federation for East Timor.

East Timor Religious Outreach (ETRO) • 1600 Clay St, San Francisco CA 94109 • 415 474 6219 • email: *easttim@jps.net*

Canadian Action for Indonesia and East Timor (CAFIET) • PO Box 562, Station P, Toronto, Ontario M5S 2T1 Canada • 416 531 5850 • fax: 416 588 5556 • email: *cafiet@interlog.com*

East Timor Alert Network (ETAN/Canada) • PO Box 4115, Station E, Ottawa, Ontario, K1S 5B1 Canada • 613 230 4070 • fax: 613 230 8854 • email: *info@etan.ca*

East Timor solidarity groups in other countries
Contact ETAN/US (above) for information.

RECOMMENDED READING

So our stories have made you sad, you tell me.
Yes, this I can understand...but tears are not the
right response. For every painful story there is
one of beauty, one to learn from....You must
never forget the art of enjoyment. Otherwise
the pain of survival will crush you.

> Gaspar, a guerrilla with the Guatemalan
> National Revolutionary Union

Aditjondro, George. *Is Oil Thicker than Blood? A Study of Oil Companies' Interests and Western Complicity in Indonesia's Annexation of East Timor.* Nova Science, Commack, NY. 1999.

Dunn, James. *Timor: A People Betrayed,* Second Edition. ABC Books, Sydney, Australia. 1996.

Kohen, Arnold. *From the Place of the Dead: The Epic Struggles of Bishop Belo of East Timor.* St. Martin's Press, New York. 1999.

Pinto, Constâncio and **Matthew Jardine.** *East Timor's Unfinished Struggle: Inside the Timorese Resistance.* South End Press, Boston. 1997.

The TAPOL Bulletin (a bimonthly update on politics and human rights throughout Indonesia and East Timor). The Indonesian Human Rights Campaign, 111 Northwood Road, Thornton Heath, Surrey, CR7 8HW, United Kingdom • phone: 81 771 2904 • fax: 81 653 0322 • email: *tapol@gn.apc.org*

Turner, Michele. *Telling: East Timor Personal Testimonies 1942–1992.* New South Wales University Press, PO Box 1, Kensington NSW Australia. 1992.

All these books are available from ETAN/US
(see the previous page).   *Matthew Jardine*

N   O   T   E   S

Sources for the facts in this book are listed below by page numbers and brief subject descriptions *(in italics)*. Full publication data is given the first time a work is cited. If a work is mentioned in the *Recommended Reading* section on the facing page, it's **boldfaced** when it's first cited below; this tells you to look in that section for the publication information.

Preface

6 • *1965 massacre.* The CIA estimates the number killed at a quarter million and Indonesian state security at half a million, but Amnesty International, a much more reliable source—and one with no ax to grind—estimates "many more than one million" victims. For more on this, see Noam Chomsky, *Z Magazine*, 9/90, 15–23, and Benedict Anderson and Ruth McVey, "What Happened in Indonesia?," letter to the editor in *The New York Review*, 6/1/78, 40–42.

7 • *200,000+ dead.* Asia Watch, *Human Rights in Indonesia and East Timor,* Human Rights Watch (New York), 1989, 253.

Introduction

8 • *Anderson quote.* Tom Hyland, AAP Bureau Chief in Melbourne, article reprinted in the *Newsletter of the East Timor Talks Campaign,* Fitzroy, Australia, 9/92, reporting a talk by Anderson in Melbourne. He expressed similar views at a talk at Harvard at about the same time.

8–9 • *Western attitudes.* Geoffrey Gunn, *A Critical View of Western Scholarship and Journalism,* Manila, 1994. Most of the material has been available since the late 1970's. See Noam Chomsky and Edward S. Herman, *The Washington Connection and Third World Fascism: The Political Economy of Human Rights, Vol. 1,* South End Press (Boston),1979, and much subsequent work.

8–9 • *Woolcott cables.* Noam Chomsky, *Towards a New Cold War,* Pantheon,1982.

11 • *Great souls care little....* Aaron Burr quoted "in the manner of" Napoleon, in Henry Adams, *History of the United States of America during the Administration of Thomas Jefferson,* Library of America, 1986, 132.

13 • *Timor's petroleum smells better....* John Pilger, "Blood on the Hands of the Mates," *Green Left,* 4/20/94.

14 • *Boston Globe headline.* Story by Brian McGrory, 11/12/92.

14 • *Lloyd George quote.* See Noam Chomsky, *Year 501: The Conquest Continues,* South End, 1993, Ch. 1.

The Santa Cruz Massacre

16 • *Eyewitness report.* Allan Nairn, *The New Yorker,* 12/9/91, 41.

16 • *Hundreds killed at Santa Cruz.* National Council of Maubere Resistance (CNRM) press release, East Timor, 9/3/92.

16 • *Cold-blooded massacre.* Max Stahl, "Massacre Among the Graves," *Independent on Sunday* (London), 11/17/91.

16 • *Soldiers later kill wounded.* Max Stahl, "Dili, the bloody Aftermath," *Sydney Morning Herald,* 2/12/94.

17 • *International and Indonesian reaction to Santa Cruz.* Matthew Jardine, "Forgotten Genocide: A little attention, at last, for East Timor," *The Progressive,* 12/92, 19–20.

Portuguese rule

18 • *East Timor sits still.* José Ramos-Horta, *Funu: the Unfinished Saga of East Timor,* Red Sea Press (Trenton, NJ), 1987, 14.

18 • *Portuguese arrive in Timor.* Jill Jolliffe, *East Timor: Nationalism and Colonialism,* University of Queensland Press, 1978, 22–23; Taylor, John G. *Indonesia's Forgotten War: The Hidden History of East Timor.* Zed Books, London. 1991, 2–3.

18 • *Early Portuguese trade.* Jolliffe, 22–23; Taylor, 2–3, 8.

18 • *Arrival of Topasses.* **Dunn**, 13–14; C. R. Boxer, "Portuguese Timor: A Rough Island Story: 1515–1960," *History Today,* May 1960, 350.

19 • *Power struggles for control.* William Burton Sowash, "Colonial Rivalries in Timor," *The Far Eastern Quarterly,* 5/48, 230; Taylor, 4.

19 • *Official division of the island.* Taylor, 12.

19 • *Wallace describes Timor.* Alfred Russel Wallace, *The Malay Archipelago: The Land of the Orang-utan, and the Bird of Paradise,* MacMillan, vol. 1, 1869, 307.

19 • *Portugal shows new interest in East Timor.* Jolliffe, 34; Taylor, 10.

19 • *Cash crops and forced labor.* Gerard J. Telkamp, "The Economic Structure of an Outpost in the Outer Islands in the Indonesian Archipelago: Portuguese Timor 1850– 1975," in P. Creutzberg, *Between Peoples and Statistics: Essays on Modern Indonesian History,* Martin Nijhoff, 1979, 78; G. Clarence-Smith, "Planters and Small Holders in Portuguese Timor in the 19th and 20th Centuries," *Indonesia Circle,* Mar 92, 15–30.

20 • *1910–12 revolt.* Jolliffe, 36–39; Dunn, 16–17.

20 • *Rise of Timorese elite.* Taylor, 16; Dunn, 6–7.

20 • *Catholic schools.* A. Diaz de Rábago, "Portuguese Timor," *New Catholic Encyclopedia,* Vol. 14, McGraw Hill, 1967, 166.

20 • *Dili economically backward.* Dunn, 18.

World War II and after

21 • *Japanese invasion and occupation.* Dunn, 19–20; **Turner**, 3.

21 • *Shouachi's memories.* Quoted in Turner, 52.

21–22 • *Japan might have ignored Timor.* Dunn, 19–22; Turner, 4; Taylor, 14.

22 • *Portuguese Timor rebuilt.* Taylor, 14.

22 • *Serious revolt.* Taylor, 21; Jolliffe, 48–49; Dunn, 28–29

22 • *Church encourages patriotism.* Dunn, 45.

23 • *US assists Indonesian independence.* Malcolm Caldwell, "Oil and Imperialism in East Asia," *Journal of Contemporary Asia*, No. 3, 1971, 22.

23 • *Mass media in Portuguese Timor.* Telkamp, 77; Dunn, 35.

23 • *Jesuit education.* Dunn, 46–47; Taylor, 27.

24 • *Dissidents meet clandestinely.* Jolliffe, 55–56.

The struggle for independence

24 • *Murdani quote.* Speech translated and distributed by **TAPOL**.

25 • *MFA's attitude to colonies.* Taylor, 25.

25 • *Three options for Timor.* Dunn, 52.

25 • *No Portuguese action on options.* Helen Hill, *FRETILIN: The Origins, Ideologies and Strategies of a Nationalist Movement in East Timor*, M.A. Thesis, Monash University, Australia, 1978, 113.

25 • *UDT formed.* Taylor, 26; Ramos-Horta, 29–31; Dunn, 53–54.

25 • *ASDT formed.* Dunn, 56; Ramos-Horta, 35; Taylor, 27.

26 • *UDT and ASDT leaders.* Jolliffe, 69; Taylor 27; Dunn, 53, 56–57.

26 • *APODETI and Indonesian intelligence.* Taylor, 23, 27–28; Dunn, 63–64.

26–27 • *UDT loses ground to the ASDT.* Dunn, 55.

27 • *Foreign minister Malik reassures Ramos-Horta.* Ramos-Horta, 41–43; Dunn, 58–59; Taylor, 29. For a copy of Malik's letter, see Jolliffe, 66.

27 • *Australia fails to support independence.* Dunn, 59–60; Ramos-Horta, 75–77; Taylor 29–30.

27 • *FRETILIN'S program.* Taylor, 42; Ramos-Horta, 37.

27 • *FRETILIN most popular party.* Dunn, 61–62; Taylor, 35; Jolliffe, 89–90.

27 • *Lisbon calls independence unrealistic.* Dunn, 76–77; Taylor, 36–37.

27–28 • *Coalition formed and APODETI rejects MFA offer.* [Helen] Hill, 115–16; Taylor, 38–39.

28 • *Outcome of first decolonization talk.* Taylor, 39; Jolliffe, 113.

28 • *Operation Komodo.* Dunn, 78; Taylor, 31.

28 • *Gough Whitlam quote.* Sinar Harapan (Jakarta), 9/74, quoted in Taylor, 32.

28 • *Whitlam's comments favorable to Indonesia.* Dunn, 98–99, Taylor, 32.

28 • *Komodo intensified.* Taylor, 39–40.

29 • *Komodo succeeds in breaking up coalition.* Jolliffe, 115–16; Taylor, 41–43, 46.

29 • *UDT coup.* Taylor, 50–51; Jolliffe, 115–19.

29 • *UDT driven into West Timor.* Carmel Budiardjo & Liem Soei Liong, *The War Against East Timor,* Zed Books, 1984, 55; Taylor, 51; Dunn, 159; Jolliffe, chapter 4.

29 • *Refugees forced to support* integration. Jolliffe, 145.

29 • *UDT leader not wanting to sign petition.* Dunn, 160.

30 • *People support* de facto *government.* Dunn, 186–87.

30 • *Portugal postpones peace talks.* Ramos-Horta, 58–59.

30 • *CIA confirms Indonesian aggression.* Dale Van Atta and Brian Toohey. "The Timor Papers" (Parts I & II), *The National Times* (Australia), 5/30–6/5; 6/6–12, 1982.

30 • *ABRI attacks East Timorese towns.* Budiardjo & Liem, 20–21.

30–31 • *Recognition comes slowly.* Jolliffe, 216–17.

Indonesia invades

31 • *FRETILIN broadcast.* Quoted in Budiardjo & Liem, 1984, 15

31 • *Malik minimalizes East Timorese losses.* AAP-Reuter dispatch from Jakarta, *Canberra Times,* 4/1/77, quoted in Chomsky & Herman, 176.

31–32 • *Catholic bishop reports killing everywhere. TAPOL Bulletin,* Sep 83.

32 • *Eloise's report.* Turner, 107.

32–33 • *Mr. Siong's report.* Turner. 104–5.

33 • *ABRI looting.* Taylor, 69–70; Dunn, 253.

33 • *Olinda's report.* Turner, 146–47.

33–34 • *ABRI rape and abuse East Timorese women.* Dunn, 253.

34 • *Edhina's report.* Turner, 109–10.

34 • *Anti-Chinese sentiment.* Taylor, 69; Andrew McMillan, *Death in Dili,* Hodder & Stoughton, Rydalmere NSW Australia, 1992, 67.

35 • *Invasion expands and number of East Timorese killed.* Budiardjo & Liem, 1984, 15, 23; Taylor, 71; Dunn, 259–60, 302–303.

35 • *Indonesia-staged event.* Dunn, 263–64; Taylor, 73–74.

35 • *Eyewitness account of People's Assembly.* Hamish McDonald, "Staging the Rites of Integration," *Far Eastern Economic Review,* 6/18/76, 22.

UN response to the invasion

36 • *UN voting.* Arnold Kohen and JohnTaylor, *An Act of Genocide: Indonesia's Invasion of East Timor,* London: TAPOL, 1979, 38; Antonio Barbedo de Magalhaees, *Timor-Leste: Mensagem Aos Vivos,* LIMIAR (Porto, Brazil), 1983, 263–68.

36 • *Ramos-Horta explains voting discrepancies.* Ramos-Horta, 112.

37 • *Roger Clark's analysis.* Phone conversation between Professor Clark and author, 8/17/93.

37 • *Moynihan quote.* Daniel P. Moynihan (with Suzanne Weaver), *A Dangerous Place,* Little, Brown & Co., 1978, 247.

US support for Indonesia

37 • *Bush on Iraqi invasion.* Quoted in Noam Chomsky, "Nefarious Aggression," *Z Magazine,* 10/90, 19.

37 • *Donald Keough quote.* Quoted in *Dollars and Sense* (Somerville, MA), 5/92, 4.

38 • *Cable from Australia's ambassador. Sun* (Melbourne, Australia), 5/1/76, quoted in Kohen and Taylor, 34–35.

38 • *Kissinger in Jakarta. Los Angeles Times,* 12/7/75.

38 • *US approval of invasion.* Jack Anderson, "Another Slaughter," *San Francisco Chronicle,* 11/9/79, 61.

38–39 • *US State Department condones invasion.* Ross Waby, "Aid to Indonesia Doubled as US Shrugs off Timor," *The Australian,* 1/22/76.

39 • *US trade with Dutch East Indies.* Julie Southwood and Patrick Flanagan, *Indonesia: Law, Propaganda and Terror,* Zed Books, 1983, 22–23.

39 • *Indonesia supplies 15 commodities.* Jonathan Marshall, "Southeast Asia and US-Japan Relations: 1940–1941," *Pacific Research & World Empire Telegram,* 3–4/73, 7.

39 • *Japan's defeat boon to US economy.* US Congress, Naval Affairs, and Merchant Marine and Fisheries Committees, "No. 67: Survey of Pacific Areas," *Report to Chairman,* 5/29/46, 2, quoted in Peter Hayes, Lyuba Zarsky and Walden Bello, *American Lake: Nuclear Period in the Pacific,* Penguin, 1986, 20–21.

39–40 • *Kennan's advice.* George F. Kennan, "Review of Current Trends, US Foreign Policy," PPS/23, Top Secret. Included in *Foreign Relations of the United States, 1948,* vol. 1, part 2, Government Printing Office, 1976, 509–29.

40 • *Nixon quotes.* Peter Dale Scott, "Exporting Military-Economic Development: America and the Overthrow of Sukarno," in Malcolm Caldwell, ed., *Ten Years' Military Terror in Indonesia,* Bertrand Russell Peace Foundation for Spokesman Books (UK), 1975, 241; Richard M. Nixon, "Asia After Viet Nam," *Foreign Affairs,* 10/67, 111.

40 • *US devastates Indochina.* Noam Chomsky, *Turning the Tide: US Intervention in Central America and the Struggle for Peace,* South End, 1985, 216–17; Marilyn Young, *The Vietnam Wars 1945–1990,* Harper, 1991, 301–302.

40 • *US supports Indonesian independence and curries favor with Indonesian army.* Carmel Budiardjo, *Indonesia: Mass Extermination and the Consolidation of Authoritarian Power* in Alexander George, ed., *Western State Terrorism,* Cambridge (UK), Polity Press, 1991; Caldwell, 22.

40–41 • *Suharto's slaughter, and US Embassy supplies names.* Benedict Anderson and Ruth McVey, "What Happened in Indonesia," letter to the editor in *The New York Review,* 6/1/78, 42; Noam Chomsky, "'A Gleam of Light in Asia,'" *Z Magazine,* 9/90, 15–17.

41 • Suharto open to US investment. Carmel Budiardjo & Liem Soei Liong, *West Papua: The Obliteration of a People,* Surrey (UK), TAPOL, the Indonesian Human Rights Campaign, 1988, 33.

41 • US investment in Indonesia. Mark Selden, "American Global Enterprise and Asia," *Bulletin of Concerned Asian Scholars,* 4–6/ 75, 24.

41 • US companies supply 90% of weapons for invasion. Chomsky and Herman, 144–45.

41–42 • US military assistance. William D. Hartung & Jennifer Washburn, "U.S. Arms Transfers to Indonesia 1975–97: Who's Influencing Whom?" World Policy Institute (New York), 3/97, 4–8; Arnold Kohen and Roberta Quance, "The Politics of Starvation," *Inquiry,* 2/18/90, 20–21; Taylor, 169.

42 • ABRI officers trained in US. Charles Scheiner, "No US Military Aid to Indonesia in Fiscal Year 1993!" *Bulletin of Concerned Asian Scholars,* 7–9/92, 51.

42 • State Department explains friendly relations with Indonesia. Waby.

42 • Reporting on East Timor declines. Chomsky and Herman; Taylor, 71.

42–43 • Los Angeles Times reporting. Matthew Jardine, "East Timor: Media Ignored Genocide," *Extra!,* 11–12/93.

43 • JCET training. Allan Nairn, "Indonesia's Killers," *The Nation,* 3/30/98, 6–7.

44 • Albright praises Suharto. Philip Shenon, "US Officials Say Indonesia Has to Look Beyond Suharto's Successor and the Military," *The New York Times,* 5/21/98.

Australian support for Indonesia

44 • Hawke on Iraqi invasion. Reuters, "Australian Warships Sail for Persian Gulf Amid Protests," dateline: Sydney, Australia, 8/13/90.

44 • Fewer Timorese than Indonesians. Quoted in Dunn, 124.

45 • Woolcott cable to Canberra. Bruce Juddery, "Envoy Puts Jakarta's View," *Canberra Times,* 1/16/76

45 • Fraser undermines FRETILIN. Kohen & Taylor, 105–7.

45 • Australian military assistance. Senate Standing Committee on Foreign Affairs and Defence of the Parliament of the Commonwealth of Australia, *Australia's Defence Co-operation with its Neighbours in the Asian-Pacific Region,* Australian Government Publishing Service, 1984.

46 • Ford administration pressures Australia. Michael Richardson, "Fraser given blunt warning at Washington talks: 'Don't anger Jakarta'—US protecting Indon channel for its N-subs," *The Age* (Melbourne), 8/3/76, 1.

46 • Australian Defense Department paper. J. R. Walsh & George Munster, *Documents on Australian Defence and Foreign Policy, 1968–1975,* J.R. Walsh and G. J. Munster (Hong Kong), 1980, 22.

46 • *Whitlam's foreign policy goal. National Times,* 7/19–24/76, quoted in Kohen & Taylor, 103.

46 • *Timor Gap oil field. TAPOL Bulletin,* 2/90, 18.

46–47 • *Woolcott's advice to Canberra.* Walsh & Munster, 197–200.

47 • *Timor Gap probably illegal.* Roger Clark, "Timor Gap: the Legality of the Treaty on the Zone of Cooperation in an Area Between the Indonesian Province of East Timor and Northern Australia," *Pace Yearbook of Internaional Law,* Vol. 4:69, 1992, 69–95.

47 • *Australia-Indonesia security accord.* Dunn, 348–49.

Other supporters of Indonesia

48 • *Suharto's 1975 visit to Canada.* Scharfe, Sharon. *Complicity: Human Rights and Canadian Foreign Policy: The Case of East Timor.* Black Rose Books, Montreal, 1996. 130–33

48–49 • *Canadian trade and investment in Indonesia.* Department of Foreign Affairs and International Trade (Canadian gov.), *CanadExport,* 1995; Canadian Embassy (Jakarta) website, http://www.dfait-maeci.gc.ca/jakarta/menu-e.htm?politik-e.htm.

48–49 • *Canadian weapons in East Timor.* José Ramos-Horta, *Funu.*

49 • *Canadian arms exports.* Figures provided by Sharon Scharfe of Parlamentarians for East Timor in Ottawa (pet@web.net) and based on Foreign Ministry documents obtained through Canada's Access of Information Act.

49 • *Japan second leading investor in Indonesia.* Selden, 24.

49 • *Japan leading investor in Indonesia.* Walden Bello, *People and Power in the Pacific: the Struggle for the Post-Cold War Order,* Pluto Press (London) , 1992, 84.

49 • *Japan leading aid-giver to Jakarta.* "Double Standard! Japan's Stand on East Timor," paper presented by the Free East Timor Japan Coalition to the UN World conference on Human Rights, 6/93, 2.

49 • *Japan's aid charter and 1996 aid.* From Japanese Foreign Ministry's website, http://www.mofa.go.jp/policy/oda/summary/1997.

50 • *Japan's Diplomatic White Paper.* Quoted in Akihisa Matsuno, "Japan and the East Timor Issue: The Government, Citizens' Movement and Public Opinion," paper prepared for the 5th Symposium of Oporto University on East Timor, Portugal, 7/22–29/93, 2.

50 • *British ambassador's advice to Foreign Office.* Walsh & Munster, 192–93.

50–51 • *British assistance to Indonesia.* TAPOL, *Indonesia: The British Perspective,* 1993.

51 • *Continued British arms sales and investments.* TAPOL, "Ethics, Investments and Repression—Britain and Indonesia: The Test for Government and Business," 3/31/98.

51 • *IGGI aid.* G.A. Posthumus, *The Inter Governmental Group on Indonesia (I.G.G.I.),* Rotterdam, Rotterdam Univ. Press, 1971; Budiardjo & Liem, 1988, 114; Taylor, 75–76.

51 • *CGI aid.* Christopher Noble, "Donors throw $7.9 bln lifeline to Indonesia," Reuters (dateline Paris), 7/30/98.

51 • *Indonesia's external debt.* World Bank website, http://www.cdinet.com/DEC/wdi98/new/countrydata/aag/idn_aag.pdf.

Indonesia's war of occupation

52 • *ABRI limited to major towns.* Taylor, 70–71.

52 • *ABRI progresses slowly in rural areas.* Van Atta and Toohey, 6/6–12/82; Budiardjo & Liem, 1984, 23.

52 • *Indonesian casualties in first weeks of invasion.* "Jakarta's Timor Dead...," *Washington Post,* 1/9/76.

52 • *Four-month ABRI death toll.* Taylor, 70.

52–53 • *FRETILIN preparations and life in liberated areas.* Budiardjo & Liem, 1984, 57–59; Taylor, 70–71.

53 • *Encirclement and annihilation tactics.* Budiardjo & Liem, 1984, 27; Taylor, 85.

53–54 • *Lourenço's report.* Turner, 113–14.

54 • *Additional Western military sales and FALINTIL units surrender.* Taylor, 86–87; Budiardjo & Liem, 1984, 66.

54–55 • *Xavier's report.* Turner, 119–20.

55 • *Civilian deaths.* Taylor, 88.

55 • *FRETILIN's losses.* Budiardjo & Liem, 1984, 67.

55 • *Relocation and deportation.* Taylor, 85.

56 • *Gusmão successfully reorganizes FRETILIN.* Taylor, 115–16; Budiardjo & Liem, 1984, 67–69, 71.

56 • *FRETILIN regains territory.* Taylor, 115–16; Budiardjo & Liem, 1984, 68–71.

56–57 • *da Costa's report.* Turner, 185–86.

56–57 • *"fence of legs".* Taylor, 117–20.

57–58 • *FRETILIN-ABRI cease-fire.* Taylor, 136–37; Budiardjo & Liem, 1984, 72–73.

58 • *Murdani breaks cease-fire. Sinar Harapan,* 8/17/83, quoted in Taylor, 142.

58 • *FRETILIN consolidates underground network.* Budiardjo & Liem, 1984, 72–73, Taylor, 136–37.

58 • *ABRI offensive and withdrawal.* Budiardjo & Liem, 1984, 141–43; Taylor, 141–42, 160

58 • *Military situation stalemated.* Taylor, 160–61.

You're Indonesians, damn it!

59 • *Military commander explains Indonesianization.* Budiardjo & Liem, 1984, 98.

59–60 • *ACFOA quote.* Quoted in Kohen and Taylor, 88.

60 • *Results of forced relocation.* Taylor, 97.

60 • *Forced labor in camps.* Kohen and Taylor, 84–88.

60 • *ABRI undermines traditional social organization.* Taylor, 92–93.

60 • *Babinsas. TAPOL Bulletin,* No. 59, 1983.

61 • *Justino describes resettlement villages.* Turner, 178.

61 • *Indonesia takes over former Portuguese enterprises and traditionally held lands.* Budiardjo & Liem, 1984, 106; Dr. Mubyarto and Dr. Loekaman Soetrisno et al., *East Timor: The Impact of Integration: an Indonesian Socio-Anthropological Study,* Indonesia Resources and Information Program (IRIP), 1991, 20; Turner, 193; Taylor, 123.

62 • *Switch to Indonesian land tenure.* "Timorese Convert to Indonesian Land Certificates," *Inside Indonesia,* 3/91.

62 • *Monopoly lands with marines.* Barry Wain, "Military Seen Behind Firm Controlling Timor's Coffee," *Asian Wall Street Journal,* 6/16/82, 1.

62 • *Denok diversifies.* Budiardjo & Liem, 1984, 106.

62 • *Sandalwood monopoly.* Wain, 3.

62 • *PT Batara Indra.* George J. Aditjondro. *In the Shadow of Mount Ramelau: The Impact of the Occupation of East Timor,* Lieden (The Netherlands), Indonesian Documentation and Information Centre, 1994, 58–62.

63 • *Denok's power declining.* Based on interviews in East Timor conducted by the author in 1996 and 1998.

63 • *Indonesians replace ethnic-Chinese in economy.* Hadi M. Soesastro, "East Timor: Questions of Economic Viability." in Hal Hill, ed., *Unity and Diversity: Regional Economic Development in Indonesia since 1970,* Oxford Univ. Press, 1989, 215; Adam Kaye, "East Timor Depends on Jakarta's Largesse," *Far Eastern Economic Review,* 8/8/85, 20–23.

63 • *Local production replaced by Indonesian imports.* Taylor,127.

63 • *Anthropological study warning and follow-up.* Mubyarto et al., 51.

63–64 • *Schools emphasize things Indonesian.* Budiardjo & Liem, 1984, 111.

64 • *Physical education and* Pramuka. Taylor, 129; Budiardjo & Liem, 1984, 109–113.

64 • *Refugee testimony.* Quoted in Taylor, 128.

64 • *Indonesians increase schools.* Department of Information, *The Province of East Timor: Development in Progress,* Republic of Indonesia, 1980.

64 • *Illiteracy remains high. Jakarta Post,* 8/5/89, cited in Taylor, 129.

64 • *Birth control program.* Quoted in Taylor, 159.

65 • *Forced sterilization of women.* Taylor, 158; *TAPOL Bulletin,* 9/83, 8.

65 • *Belo denies population problem.* Asia Watch, 74.

65 • *Objectives and practices of transmigration.* Marcus Colchester, "The Struggle for Land—Tribal Peoples in the Face of the Transmigration Programme," *The Ecologist,* vol. 16, no. 2/3, 1986, 103; Taylor, 124; Aditjondro, 26.

65 • Transmigration figures through 1993. João Mariano de Sousa Saldanha, *The Political Economy of East Timor Development,* Pusatka Sinar Harapan, Jakarta, 1994, 355.

65–66 • Voluntary migrants. Mariel Otten, "'Transmigrasi': From Poverty to Bare Subsistence," *The Ecologist,* 16/2–3, 1986, 74–75.

66 • 150,000 Indonesian settlers. Peter Carey, "The Forging of a Nation: East Timor," in Peter Carey and G. Carter Bentley (eds.), *East Timor at the Crossroads: The Forging of a Nation,* University of Hawaii Press in association with the Social Science Research Council, New York and Honolulu, 1995, 2.

66 • Migrants marginalizing indigenous population. Barbara Crossette, "New Migrants Altering Face of East Timor," *The New York Times,* 10/30/94, 4; Mubyarto et al., 51–52.

66 • East Timorese forced to join ABRI. Dunn, 268–69; Budiardjo & Liem, 1984, Part II; Human Rights Watch/Asia, "Deteriorating Human Rights in East Timor," 9/97.

66–67 • Jorge's story. Turner, 172–74.

Developments since Santa Cruz and future prospects

00 • Portugal's support for East Timor. Taylor, 171–74; Pat Walsh, "Towards a Just Peace," in Carey and Bentley, 150–51.

00 • APEC protests. Matthew Jardine, "APEC, the United States & East Timor," *Z Magazine,* 1/95, 34–39.

00 • Paramilitary terror. Aniceto Guterres Lopes, "East Timor's Bloodiest Tradition," *The New York Times,* 5/5/99; Keith Richburg. "A Campaign of Terror," *The Washington Post,* 5/9/99, A18; and Allan Nairn, "License to Kill in Timor," *The Nation,* 5/31/99.

00 • Habibie allows for independence. TAPOL Bulletin 151, 3/99.

My visits to East Timor

00 • "Slaves of the Indonesians." Matthew Jardine, "The Secret Sacrifice of East Timor: Amid Invasion, Massacre, and Insurrection, the Church Takes a Stand," *Christianity & Crisis,* 2/1/93, 16–18.

00 • 1996 visit. Matthew Jardine, "In East Timor, Teetering On the Edge of More Bloodshed," *The Washington Post,* 3/2/97, C3.

00 • Meeting with David Alex. Matthew Jardine, "The US-Indonesia Alliance Against East Timor," *The Christian Science Monitor,* 1/14/97.

00 • David Alex killed. Matthew Jardine, "The Life and Death of David Alex and the Ongoing Struggle for East Timor," *Cultural Survival Quarterly,* 21/3, Fall '97, 42–45.

Recommended reading

77–78 • Gaspar quote. Jennifer Harbury, *Bridge of Courage: Life Stories of the Guatemalan Compañeros and Compañeras,* Common Courage Press (Monroe ME), 1994, 81.

I N D E X